30-SECOND
NEW YORK

30-SECOND
NEW YORK

The 50 key visions, events and
architects that shaped the city,
each explained in half a minute

Editor
Sarah Fenton

Contributors
Sarah Fenton
Cheong Kim
Andrew Kryzak
Matthew Gordon Lasner
Chris McNickle
Christopher Mitchell
Patrick Nugent
Nancy Green Saraisky
Aaron Shkuda
Jennifer Shalant
Michael Willoughby

Illustrations
Nicky Ackland-Snow

IVY PRESS

First published in the UK in 2017 by
Ivy Press
Ovest House
58 West Street
Brighton BN1 2RA
United Kingdom
www.quartoknows.com

British Library Cataloguing-in-
Publication Data
A catalogue record for this
book is available from the
British Library.

ISBN: 978-1-78240-453-8

This book was conceived,
designed and produced by
Ivy Press

Publisher **Susan Kelly**
Creative Director **Michael Whitehead**
Editorial Director **Tom Kitch**
Art Director **James Lawrence**
Project Editor **Jamie Pumfrey**
Designer **Ginny Zeal**
Commissioning Editor **Sophie Collins**
Glossaries **Charles Phillips**

Typeset in Section

Printed in China

10 9 8 7 6 5 4 3 2 1

CONTENTS

INTRODUCTION
Sarah Fenton

New York City's only humble feature is its origin story: this is a place created by accident. When Henry Hudson sailed into what is now New York Harbor in September 1609, he was searching not for political, religious or even individual freedom, but for a faster trade route to China, on behalf of a multinational corporation. Plymouth, Virginia, Massachusetts and Maryland – North America's other early colonies had their differences, but all were founded as deliberate, earnest and unitary communities: culturally homogenous and overwhelmingly English. Not so New Amsterdam (as New York City was first christened). A Dutch outpost, it was a capitalist settlement with meagre and merely material ambitions. By the 1650s, it was home to a motley crew of inhabitants – Dutch, Walloons, multiracial Brazilians, French, English, Portuguese, Swedes, Finns and Jews among them – said to speak at least 18 languages and practise 'sundry' religions. The English fleet that captured (and renamed) New Amsterdam in 1664 took possession of the most disorderly and contentious village on the eastern seaboard.

Over the course of the next century, the colonies generally – and New York particularly – would develop in ways that set them increasingly at odds with the Crown. Colonial New York was competitive, fragmented and characterized by a high degree of popular participation in politics. Still, the American Revolution astonished imperial Britain and has astonished historians ever since. A window into the aftermath of that revolution can be found in Chapter 2 through the biography of Alexander Hamilton. One wonders what Hamilton – immigrant, lover of commerce and cities – would have made of the unparalleled rates of immigration, industrialization and urbanization that characterized his city during the late nineteenth century. By the end of that century, New York was the fastest-growing city on the globe and its Lower East Side the world's most densely inhabited neighbourhood; by 1930, it had surpassed London as the world's largest city. The cultural and financial capital of the world throughout the second half of the twentieth century, New York City is still home to the world's two largest stock exchanges – a fact that would surely have astonished Henry Hudson and the Dutch West India Company that employed him: they saw the city's financial future as limited to the international market in beaver skins.

In response to the city's dizzying pace, its sheer size and bottomless diversity, you might well ask, how can all of that fit into this slim volume? The short answer is: it can't. This book does not pretend to encyclopaedic coverage. Instead, it is a friendly introduction to the world's greatest city. Welcome to New York.

How This Book Works

30-Second New York is divided into seven chapters, each one split into anything from six to nine topics and one biography. The topics are covered in three sections: the longest, **the 30-Second Tour**, provides a narrative arc – beginning, middle and where we are now – in a condensed space. To the left lies the **3-Second Survey** summarising the topic while the **3-Minute Overview** assesses the subject's overall significance or pulls out an emblematic detail for further reflection. To the right of the **30-Second Tour**, you'll find suggestions for a few related entries perched atop two or three brief biographies of figures central to the subject. Each of these elements is a puzzle piece; putting them together page by page will give you a steady grasp of individual subjects – in many cases we'll have managed not to sate your curiosity but to stoke it, which is all for the better.

The topics in the book appear more or less chronologically, from land formation to peopling that land; then to governing the people and 'improving' the land; and finally experiencing the city, studying and entertaining it. although you don't need to read the book straight through – it's not a linear narrative. Much like life outside the pages of a book, subjects within the book overlap one another – chronologically, thematically, topically and biographically. Certain characters (Teddy Roosevelt, say, or James Baldwin) exit the stage of one entry only to make a welcome return in another. Structures and events reappear in entries that would seem to have little in common save the city they share: the Statue of Liberty, Brooklyn Bridge and Empire State Building earn multiple mentions, as (less glowingly) do the 1863 Draft Riots.

I have a long-running debate with Edward Denison, the editor of the London edition in this series, regarding the relative merits of each other's cities. He argues well on behalf of London's historical significance and sweep; having lived in both cities, I will grant him that. The claim I would make on New York's behalf is a claim of vitality – of energy and reinvention, of the constant possibility of change. More languages are spoken here than in any other city in the world; maybe tomorrow I'll begin learning one of them. Every religion and every racial and ethnic group is represented here: it is the superlative urban laboratory, an experiment to discover whether all the world's peoples can live side by side in a single place. To step outside your cramped, overpriced, possibly roach-infested New York City apartment is to wonder if the man hurrying beside you in the sober grey suit could tear his shirt off at any moment to reveal a superhero's cape beneath it. There – see that girl looking lonesome on a Central Park bench? She might burst suddenly into song, as if all of life really were a musical. Anything can happen here. So much already has, much of it captured, however fleetingly, in the pages of this book.

THE LAND

THE LAND
GLOSSARY

Bronx Zoo The largest metropolitan zoo in the United States, covering 107 ha (265 acres) in Bronx Park, the Bronx. It was opened in 1899 on land sold to the city by Fordham University, with 843 animals. Today there are around 4,000.

Central Park The most visited urban park in the United States, covering 341 ha (832 acres) in middle to upper Manhattan. It was initially formed in 1857 and expanded and remodelled from 1858 onwards by Frederick Law Olmsted and Calvert Vaux. It is an iconic NY setting and has featured in more than 300 movies, making it the most filmed location in the world.

Coney Island Southwestern part of the borough of Brooklyn, on the Atlantic Ocean, known for its boardwalk, beaches and varied amusement parks. The name is thought to come from Dutch or Gaelic words for rabbit, since the area had a large rabbit population.

Flatbush A low-lying neighbourhood in Brooklyn, founded in 1651 by Dutch colonists. Flatbush was home to the celebrated Ebbets Field baseball stadium, home in 1913–57 to the Brooklyn Dodgers, but demolished in 1960.

Fordham University A private research university with three campuses – Rose Hill in the Bronx, Lincoln Center in Manhattan and Westchester in Harrison, Westchester County, New York. It was established by the Catholic Diocese of New York as St John's College in 1841. Notable alumni include Andrew Cuomo, New York state overnor from 2011 onwards, businessman and politician Donald Trump and actors Denzel Washington and Alan Alda.

Great Migration Movement of African Americans from rural areas in the South to New York, Chicago and other Northern and Midwestern cities. Around 6 million African Americans made the journey in 1910–70.

John F. Kennedy International Airport Formerly known as New York International Airport, situated in Queens. Opened in 1948, it was generally called Idlewild Airport until it was renamed in honour of President Kennedy after his assassination in 1963.

Kill Van Kull A stretch of tidal waters 305 m (1,000 ft) wide and 4.8 km (3 miles) in length between Staten Island and Bayonne, New Jersey, linking Upper New York Bay and Newark Bay. It is spanned by the Bayonne Bridge, which opened in 1931. Its name derives from a seventeenth-century Dutch phrase meaning a water channel near a ridge.

Manhattan College An independent Roman Catholic liberal arts college established on Canal Street, Manhattan, in 1853 by the Brothers of the Christian Schools. The college moved to Riverdale in the Bronx, in 1922. Notable alumni include Rudy Giuliani, former Mayor of New York.

Mannahatta The indigenous Lenape Indians' name for the site of New York, meaning 'island of many hills', which gives its name to Manhattan. Robert Juet, an officer on English explorer Henry Hudson's *Half Moon*, noted the name in his exploration of the Hudson River in 1609.

New York Botanical Garden 100 ha (250 acres) of botanical garden in the Bronx, opened in 1891 mostly on land previously owned by tobacco manufacturer Pierre Lorillard (1833–1901).

LaGuardia Airport (formerly New York Municipal) An International airport in the northern part of Queens, known as LaGuardia since 1953 in honour of former Mayor of New York, Fiorello LaGuardia. Its facilities are notoriously outdated and it is due to be completely replaced by a new airport under plans announced by Governor Andrew Cuomo in July 2015.

Rockaway Beach An ocean-side neighbourhood in the borough of Queens, containing the largest urban beach in the United States on the south shore of Long Island. Because of the area's substantial Irish-American population, the beach was once known as the 'Irish Riviera'. It was immortalized by the New York punk band the Ramones in their 1977 song 'Rockaway Beach'. It was very badly damaged by Hurricane Sandy.

Verrazano Bridge Suspension bridge that connects Staten Island and Brooklyn, crossing the Narrows, the stretch of water that connects the Upper Bay and the Lower Bay. It is named after Florentine explorer Giovanni da Verrazzano (whose surname is misspelt, with one z, in the bridge name), the first European to enter New York Harbor, in 1524. It was built in 1959–64 and designed by Othmar Ammann, designer of the George Washington Bridge. The New York City marathon begins from the Staten Island end of the bridge.

THE CITY TAKES SHAPE

the 30-second tour

Way before Brooklyn was cool, and before New Amsterdam became New York, thousands of metres of ice covered the future metropolis. New York began to emerge from the Ice Age 18,000 years ago, and it wasn't long before human visitors arrived. But the city's story doesn't begin there – the bedrock that underlies it ranges from 1.1 billion to 190 million years in age. Appropriately for a city where the old and new commingle, visitors to Central Park, Prospect Park, the New York Botanical Garden and other parks can see physical remnants of the geological past in the form of schist embankments, glacial boulders and other natural features rooted in an ancient mountain chain. Landscape ecologists with the New York-based Wildlife Conservation Society recently studied the city's ecological past, and found that for thousands of years before Europeans arrived in 1609 – back when the city was nicknamed *Mannahatta* by its Lenape people – bears, wolves, birds and salamanders roamed the landscape of hills, valleys, forests, freshwater wetlands and salt marshes, ponds and streams, with porpoises and whales spouting in the harbour.

RELATED ENTRIES
See also
THE COLONISTS TAKE
MANNAHATTA
page 34

WATERWAYS
page 70

3-SECOND SURVEY
New York's skyline springs from a durable bedrock foundation that originated 500–400 million years ago and is used in buildings and infrastructure throughout the city.

3-MINUTE OVERVIEW
The last glacial period in North America locked the New York City area under the Labrador ice sheet 20,500 years ago. As the ice melted, rising tides created the city's archipelago. Geologic forces underlie the city we know today, including a rocky band of parks and cemeteries stretching from Brooklyn into Queens, at what was once the glacier's edge. Where the land becomes flatter (for example, in Flatbush, Brooklyn) sit low-lying neighbourhoods and outwash beaches, such as Coney Island.

3-SECOND BIOGRAPHY
THEODORE ROOSEVELT SNR
1831–78
Father of the 26th United States President Teddy Roosevelt (1901–09), Theodore Senior ('Thee') was a cofounder of the Metropolitan Museum of Art as well as the American Museum of Natural History

30-SECOND TEXT
Jennifer Shalant

Visitors to New York's monumental American Museum of Natural History can take a glimpse into the past and experience models of the long-ago wildlife residents.

THE BRONX

the 30-second tour

Named for seventeenth-century

Swedish immigrant Jonas Bronck, the Bronx
– the only borough on the mainland – was a
patchwork of farms in Westchester County until
the arrival of steamships and railroads in the mid
nineteenth century. The West Bronx was the
first area outside of Manhattan annexed by
the city, in 1874, followed by the East Bronx in
1898. Manhattan College, Fordham and other
campuses in the eastern hills established the
Bronx as a 'borough of universities'. The Bronx's
history has truly been determined by the cultural
richness of its immigrants: Germans, Irish,
Italians, Poles, Russians, Eastern and Central
European Jews, African Americans, Puerto
Ricans, Jamaicans and Dominicans. In 1891, the
New York Botanical Garden opened, followed in
1899 by the Bronx Zoo. Begun in 1948, the Cross
Bronx Expressway isolated the South Bronx at
a time when industrial jobs began to dry up.
Pollution and fires gutted the neighbourhood,
which in the 1970s became a symbol for urban
decay. Nonetheless, hip hop emerged in local
house parties, where DJ Kool Herc helped invent
the genre. Since then, activists for racial and
environmental justice led by Majora Carter
have built community gardens, established
food cooperatives and led environmental
stewardship programmes to revive the area.

3-SECOND SURVEY

Its gritty reputation
notwithstanding, New
Yorkers know the Bronx for
its vibrant neighbourhoods
and the natural sanctuaries
of its shining harbours,
steep cliffs and rolling hills.

3-MINUTE OVERVIEW

During the late 1990s,
policymakers planned to
install a facility in the South
Bronx to process nearly
half of the city's waste.
A coterie of activists from
the South Bronx, a mostly
working-class Latino and
African-American
community, successfully
defeated the scheme in
2001. Activist Majora
Carter founded Sustainable
South Bronx the same year.
The South Bronx is now at
the cutting edge of the
'green economy', planting
urban farms, reclaiming
waterfronts and building
green spaces.

RELATED ENTRIES

See also
THE CITY TAKES SHAPE
page 14

GRIDLOCK ALERT
page 76

NEW YORK'S TOP 40
page 140

3-SECOND BIOGRAPHIES

JONAS BRONCK
1600–43
Swedish immigrant to New
Netherland after whom the
Bronx is named

DJ KOOL HERC
1955–
Jamaican-born DJ (birth name:
Clive Campbell), identified as a
founder of the hip-hop musical
genre in the Bronx in the 1970s

30-SECOND TEXT
Christopher Mitchell

*Despite being the third
most densely populated
county in the United
States, nearly a quarter
of the Bronx is open
space – including
the Botanical Garden
and Bronx Zoo.*

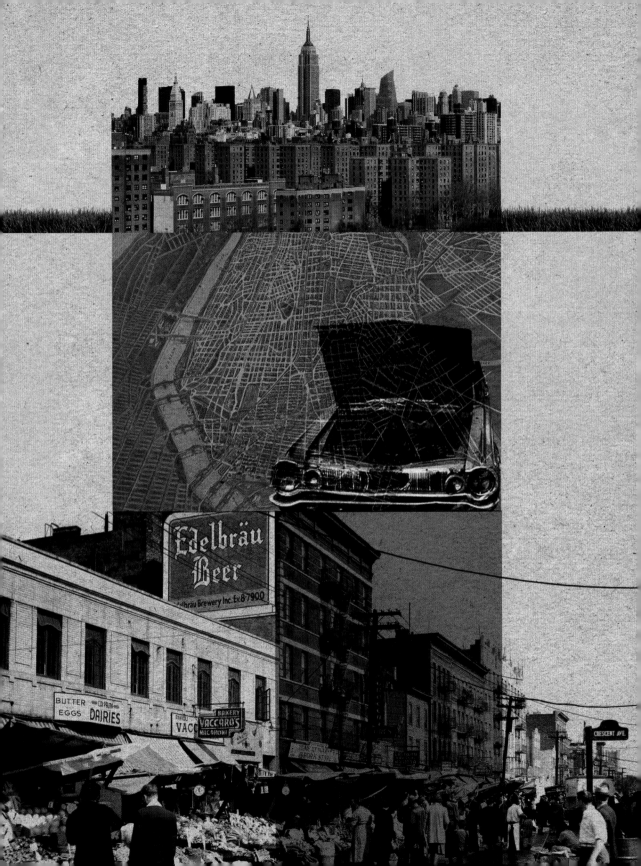

BROOKLYN

the 30-second tour

New York City's most populous borough did not become one until 1898. Its earliest inhabitants – Munsee-speaking Lenape Indians – were displaced by violence, disease and disenfranchisement, meted out by a Dutch West India Company drawn to the area's natural harbours and fertile landscape. During the eighteenth and nineteenth centuries, proximity to Manhattan proved a mixed blessing for the city of Brooklyn – the name was anglicized under English governance. The first commuter suburb, it nevertheless maintained a feisty independence: the Brooklyn Academy of Music was opened in 1859 by citizens refusing to rely on Manhattan for cultural enrichment. By the century's end, they had bowed to the inevitable, and on 1 January 1898 a municipal charter decreed that the 'City of New York' be formed of five constituent boroughs: Brooklyn, Queens, Staten Island, the Bronx and Manhattan. Prosperity in the mid twentieth century saw Brooklyn's population peak at 2.7 million but this didn't last: production declined; the beloved Brooklyn Dodgers departed. Still, a dearth of 'development' laid the groundwork for a stunning twenty first-century turnaround that saw abandoned factories and handsome intact brownstones draw discerning gentrifiers as surely as the 'fresh, green breast of the new world' had once drawn Dutch sailors.

3-SECOND SURVEY
In 1855, nearly half of Brooklyn's residents were foreign-born. Today, teenagers half a world away wear 'Brooklyn' baseball caps as a brand signifying American cool.

3-MINUTE OVERVIEW
Bursts in Brooklyn's uneven progress followed advances in transportation. Dutch towns developed along existing Indian paths until the 1640s, when ferry service across the East River to Manhattan hastened commercial development of the neighbourhoods nearest the ferry. The Brooklyn Bridge physically linked the nation's first- and third-largest cities in 1883; the elevated railroad opened in 1885. Automobiles initially helped fill in the borough's outlying areas but eventually sped commuters on to greener, suburban pastures.

RELATED ENTRIES
See also
SHIRLEY CHISHOLM
page 60

BRIDGES & TUNNELS
page 78

3-SECOND BIOGRAPHIES
LADY DEBORAH MOODY
1586–1659
The first female landowner and only woman to start a village in colonial America led a group of religious dissenters to the town of Gravesend in New Netherland (now Brooklyn)

GEORGE GERSHWIN
1898–1937
Brooklyn-born pianist who served as a 'song plugger' for Tin Pan Alley before composing such classics as *Rhapsody in Blue* (1924) and *Porgy and Bess* (1935)

30-SECOND TEXT
Sarah Fenton

Occupying the southwestern tip of Long Island, Brooklyn is adjacent to Queens and separated from Manhattan by the East River.

MANHATTAN

the 30-second tour

Dutch colonists rechristened the 'island of hills', or the Lenape *Mannahatta*, New Amsterdam in 1625. Built with slave labour, the port became the centre of New Netherland before the British renamed it New York in 1664. By 1790, the city was the new United States's largest, and briefly hosted the federal capitol. In 1792, financiers met downtown to discuss the trade of United States. Treasury bonds, an agreement that evolved into the New York Stock Exchange. As Manhattan grew into a cramped megalopolis of refugees and immigrants, city planners attempted to improve the dense, dirty cityscape with the construction of an extensive parks system, the centrepiece being the majestic Central Park, inaugurated in 1857. In 1904, the first underground subway opened. Nineteenth-century Beaux Arts monuments gave way to a labyrinth of towers whose offices house the most powerful companies in the world – not to mention Broadway and 'Museum Mile'. During the Great Migration, millions of African Americans moved to Manhattan, transforming Harlem into the preeminent centre of Black politics, thought, literature and arts. In 1952, the United Nations established its headquarters in Midtown. Following a protracted economic crisis and the 9/11 terrorist attacks on the World Trade Center in 2001, Manhattan is again thriving.

3-SECOND SURVEY
'Manhattan crowds with their turbulent musical chorus – with varied chorus, and light of the sparkling eyes; Manhattan faces and eyes forever for me.' – Walt Whitman

3-MINUTE OVERVIEW
Alarmed by 'slum clearance' programmes that demolished historic neighbourhoods and displaced thousands, activist Jane Jacobs and community preservationists waged a battle against 'power broker' Robert Moses, an unelected city planner who wanted to raze much of lower Manhattan to make way for a highway. In 1962, Moses backed down so that today, instead of racing across a highway, Manhattanites can stroll the cobbled streets of SoHo, the centre of art and fashion in the city and, arguably, the world.

RELATED ENTRIES
See also
9/11
page 64

URBAN PLANNING
page 82

3-SECOND BIOGRAPHIES
JUAN (JAN) RODRÍGUEZ
fl c. 1613
Born in Dominican Republic; sailed aboard the *Jonge Tobias* to become first non-Indian to settle in New York

ROBERT MOSES
1888–1981
Controversial city planner responsible for New York's parkway network

JANE JACOBS
1916–2006
American journalist and urban studies activist, organizer of grassroots protests against slum clearance

30-SECOND TEXT
Christopher Mitchell

Manhattan, the second-smallest county in the United States, is home to some of the world's most visited tourist attractions.

QUEENS

the 30-second tour

3-MINUTE OVERVIEW

In late October 2012, Hurricane Sandy made landfall along Queens southern coastline in the Rockaways. Floods and fires destroyed entire city blocks, especially the neighbourhood of Breezy Point, which was virtually decimated by fires. Several Queens residents lost their lives and thousands were displaced, many permanently. Although Queens residents continue to await aid and insurance money more than three years later, the resilience of the borough has seen the beach communities along the southern shore rebound.

Built on the trails and villages of displaced Maspeth, Matinecock, Rockaway and Canarsie Native Americans, Queens was home to Dutch and English colonists as early as the 1620s. Named for the English queen Catherine of Braganza, the wife of King Charles II, Queens consisted of mostly small towns and large farms until the nineteenth century. In the antebellum period, Queens was home to the area's horse-racing tracks. The Steinway piano company built a factory in Astoria and industry crept up along the waterfront of Long Island City before the county was created a New York City borough with municipal consolidation in 1898. Connections to the Long Island Railroad, the City subway and especially the Queensboro Bridge to Manhattan led to an economic and demographic boom. The population grew from about 150,000 in 1900 to more than 1 million by 1930. In 1939, the New York Municipal Airport (now LaGuardia) began operation of commercial flights, followed by the New York International Airport (now JFK) in 1948. In 1939 and 1964, the World's Fairs brought millions of visitors to Queens. Queens also hosts the Mets baseball team, as well as the United States Open in tennis. The most ethnically diverse of the five boroughs, with nearly half the population born outside the United States, residents speak well over 100 languages.

RELATED ENTRIES

See also
WHERE THE CITY MEETS THE SEA
page 28

PLAY BALL!
page 150

3-SECOND BIOGRAPHIES
CHRISTOPHER WALKEN
1943–
A celebrated product of Queens, American actor and Oscar winner, born in Astoria

CYNDI LAUPER
1953–
Singer, actress and LGBT activist, also born in Astoria, Queens, who is celebrated above all for the songs 'Girls Just Want to Have Fun' and 'Time After Time'

30-SECOND TEXT
Christopher Mitchell

Home of both New York international airports, it is no suprise that nowhere looks more like the world's 'melting pot' than in ethnically diverse Queens.

Welcome
to Queens
"The World's Borough"

Mayor Bill de Blasio
Boro Pres. Melinda Katz

27 October 1858
Born at 26 East 20th
Street in Manhattan

1880
Graduates from Harvard
in June; enters Columbia
Law school in December

1881
Becomes youngest
member ever elected to
New York State Assembly

1898
Leads Rough Riders to
victory in the Battle of
San Juan Hill

1898
Elected 33rd Governor of
New York by margin of
1 per cent

1901
Becomes 26th president
upon the assassination of
William McKinley

1904
Construction of the
Panama Canal begins

1905
Pushes Congress to
create the Forest Service

1906
Awarded Nobel Peace
Prize for mediating
Russo-Japanese War

1908
Makes the Grand Canyon
a national monument

1909
Leaves office

1912
Forms the Progressive
(or 'Bull Moose') Party;
loses presidency to
Woodrow Wilson

6 January 1919
Dies in New York

THEODORE ROOSEVELT

New York plays so prominent a role in American political life that it's a shock that only one native New Yorker has achieved the nation's highest office. Theodore Roosevelt became the 26th president of the United States (and, at 42, its youngest) in September 1901, following the assassination of President William McKinley. Regarded with suspicion by his own party, Roosevelt embodied a set of peculiarly American contradictions: a conservative Republican who pushed for progressive reforms; an avid hunter who expanded environmental safeguards; a military hawk awarded the Nobel Peace Prize.

Born to a prominent Manhattan family, Roosevelt overcame an asthmatic, cossetted childhood to make his name as a tough guy, organizing the famed Rough Riders during the Spanish-American War. Military renown helped carry him to election as governor of New York in 1898 and vice-president two years later; as president, he renamed the executive mansion 'the White House' and hired New York architects McKim, Mead & White to add the West Wing in 1902. His combative style alienated friends and foes in Washington, but when Roosevelt returned home in 1910, New Yorkers greeted him with a ticker-tape parade on an unprecedented scale.

A big man who did not share the fears of his contemporaries' towards massive corporations or muscular diplomacy, Roosevelt saw no going back from changes wrought by the Industrial Revolution. Instead, he saw it as the federal government's job to curb industry excess. Five months into his first term, Roosevelt successfully sued to halt J. P. Morgan's monopolization of the railroads. Popularly dubbed a 'trust buster', Roosevelt is more accurately regarded as an unapologetic regulator. His attempts to redress the scandalous working conditions in early twentieth-century factories, mines and sweat shops – and provide a social-welfare system for the one in five American children working in them – came to be called the Square Deal. Regarded as a bully abroad, just as he was at home, Roosevelt advised American diplomats to 'speak softly and carry a big stick', most famously in pressing for the Panama Canal. Resisting industrialists' efforts to mine every metre of the awe-inspiring American West, Roosevelt again flexed his federal muscle in declaring the Grand Canyon a national monument in 1908. The breadth of his conservationism can be appreciated along any trail of the 93 million hectares (230 million acres) of public lands established during his presidency.

Sarah Fenton

STATEN ISLAND

the 30-second tour

More than twice the size of

Manhattan, Staten Island is a 20-minute ferry ride – just past the Statue of Liberty – from the financial district. The borough's densest and most diverse neighbourhoods can be found in its northwestern corner, from which the island's sole passenger train – the Staten Island Rapid Transit – runs 23km (14 miles) southwards, serving suburban enclaves along the borough's beach-lined eastern coast. Down the centre of the island runs a steep ridge of preserved forests, scenic overlooks and large estates. To the west, a narrow industry-lined tidal channel (the Kill Van Kull) separates the borough from New Jersey. This was the last outpost of New York City to experience urbanization. The British, taking advantage of Staten Island's undeveloped topography, built lookouts and lumber mills in the Revolutionary War; the nineteenth century saw its agricultural landscape transformed by small industrial operations and Victorian retreats. Following completion of the Verrazano Bridge in 1964, the borough's economy and population exploded. Early waves of Irish and Italian migrants from Brooklyn were followed by Russians, Liberians and Sri Lankans. In the wake of Hurricane Sandy, planners and politicians continue to debate how best to guide resilient development in the face of rising sea levels.

RELATED ENTRIES
See also
WHERE THE CITY MEETS
THE SEA
page 28

BRIDGES & TUNNELS
page 78

3-SECOND BIOGRAPHIES
ALICE AUSTEN
1866–1952
One of the first female photographers to shoot New York streetscapes; thousands of her photos are on display at her former Staten Island home, Clear Comfort

BOBBY THOMSON
1923–2010
New York Giants third baseman who hit 'the shot heard round the world' to propel his team past the Brooklyn Dodgers in the National League in 1951

30-SECOND TEXT
Patrick Nugent

3-SECOND SURVEY
Residents frustrated by municipal neglect call Staten Island 'the forgotten borough'. When it comes to tourism and large-scale development, they would prefer it to remain so.

3-MINUTE OVERVIEW
Legend has it that Staten Island became a part of New York State (rather than New Jersey) on a sailing bet made in the 1670s. Not until 1898 did Staten Island join New York City. A municipal merger supported by most residents at the time quickly lost support as the borough found itself home to a long line of undesirable operations – from jails and tuberculosis hospitals to Fresh Kills Landfill.

In the southernmost part of both the city and state of New York is Staten Island, the least populated of the five boroughs.

WHERE THE CITY MEETS THE SEA

the 30-second tour

3-SECOND SURVEY

The Coney Island boardwalk, Wall Street and Rockaway Beach are threatened by rising sea levels – and there's no guide book to help.

3-MINUTE OVERVIEW

Any city will suffer when a hurricane strikes, but New York is especially prone. The New York Bight – a bend in the open waters of the Atlantic – forms a trap for storm surges. Housing developments, hospitals, schools and power plants ring the coast. A plethora of underground facilities, like the municipal water system and subway, and a skyline marked by tall buildings and suspension bridges make an aggressive approach to tackling rising sea levels essential.

It may be called the concrete jungle, but New York is also a city of islands, a metropolis moored on the Atlantic. Its 865km (538-mile) coastline encircles the most densely populated city in the United States, one that's also highly vulnerable to the changing climate. Since 1900, more than 90 per cent of New York's wetlands have been backfilled and paved over, costing the city a crucial defence against flooding. So when Hurricane Sandy swept through on October 29, 2012, with its 130km/h (80mph) winds and record storm surges, the city was brought to its knees. Millions of residents lost power for days, and thousands of homes and businesses were destroyed. Flood maps had last been updated in 1983 – since which time the number of residents living in flood-prone areas had increased more than 80 per cent, and the number of at-risk buildings by 90 per cent. The following year, Mayor Michael Bloomberg launched a $19.5 billion rebuilding and resiliency plan. The proposal called for adaptable floodwalls, storm-surge barriers and dune systems, and revising building codes throughout the city. It is considered the most comprehensive climate-resilience programme of any city worldwide, and although expenses were steep, so were the $19 billion in damages wrought by Sandy alone.

RELATED ENTRY

See also
WATERWAYS
page 70

3-SECOND BIOGRAPHY

MICHAEL BLOOMBERG
1942–
American businessman and politician, who was Mayor of New York for three consecutive terms between 2001 and 2013

30-SECOND TEXT

Jennifer Shalant

New York City's coastline stretches a total of 840 km – it is longer than the coastlines of Miami, Boston, Los Angeles and San Francisco combined.

PEOPLING THE LAND

PEOPLING THE LAND
GLOSSARY

Beaver Street A thoroughfare in the Financial District, Lower Manhattan. It was one of the first streets named in Manhattan, in the 1660s, and celebrates the rodent whose pelts were traded by the first settlers and the native Lenape. The first Jewish synagogue was established in rented quarters on Beaver Street in the late seventeenth century.

Erie Canal The canal linking the Hudson River to Lake Erie, constructed 1817–25.

Harlem Neighbourhood in Upper Manhattan, from the 1920s a centre of African-American life, business, religion and culture. Harlem was established in 1658 as a Dutch village, named after the city of Haarlem in the Netherlands. It was the site of the Harlem Renaissance of the 1920s to mid 1930s, a cultural outpouring of African-American artists, musicians and writers.

King's College Forerunner of Columbia University, established in 1754 and named for King George II with a schoolhouse alongside Trinity Church on Broadway. Among its pupils was Gouverneur Morris, who wrote sections of the United States Constitution. King's College closed in 1776 and reopened in 1784 as Columbia.

Mason-Dixon Line Boundary surveyed by English astronomer-surveyors Charles Mason and Jeremiah Dixon in 1763–67 to end a boundary dispute between the British colonies of Maryland, Pennsylvania and Delaware. It came to be seen as the boundary between the northern and southern states and after Pennsylvania abolished slavery in 1780, it marked the limits of slavery's legality.

Mikvah Bath used for ritual bathing in Judaism.

National Association for the Advancement of Colored People Civil rights organization formed in 1909 'to ensure the political, educational, social and economic equality of rights of all persons and to eliminate racial hatred and racial discrimination' by lawyer Moorfield Storey, suffragist and journalist Mary White Ovington and author W. E. B. Du Bois, among others.

Pearl Street Street in Lower Manhattan, running from Battery Park to the Brooklyn Bridge, named from the Dutch Parelstraat and so called because of the wealth of oysters found in the East River. New York's first City Hall (under the Dutch in 1653) was at 73 Pearl Street.

San Gennaro Festival Religious celebration begun in 1926 by Italian immigrants on Mulberry Street in Little Italy to celebrate the patron saint of Naples, St Januarius. Today it is principally a street fair and celebration of Italian-American culture.

The Narrows The gateway to New York City, tidal waters separating Staten Island and Brooklyn and connecting Upper and Lower New York Bay. The Verrazano–Narrows Bridge across was erected in 1964.

Trinity Church Episcopal church close to the intersection of Broadway and Wall Street in Lower Manhattan. Established in 1697 in a different location, at the head of Wall Street, it was the first Anglican church in Manhattan. The original church was destroyed by fire during the Revolutionary War; after the war, Trinity, together with all other Anglican churches in the former British colonies, separated from the Church of England, forming the Episcopal Church. A second church begun in 1788 was demolished in 1839. Today's church, the third, was built in 1839–46. In the immediate aftermath of the 9/11 attacks shell-shocked New Yorkers took refuge inside the church from the cloud of dust and debris.

Underground Railroad Route by which slaves escaped to freedom in the nineteenth century, using a network of 'safe houses' and secret routes operated by abolitionists. There were many important stops on the 'railroad' in New York, not least the Mother African Methodist Episcopal Church (known as the 'Freedom Church') at 158 Church Street in Lower Manhattan and Plymouth Church at 75 Hicks Street, Brooklyn (dubbed the Underground Railroad's 'Grand Central Depot').

Yeshiva Educational centre for studying Jewish religious texts.

THE COLONISTS TAKE MANNAHATTA

the 30-second tour

New York, New York, née New Amsterdam, née Mannahatta – the cultural identity of this melting pot has never been fixed. When Henry Hudson sailed into the harbour in 1609, the surrounding forested landscape was home to the Lenape people. The Native Americans had lived in the region for thousands of years before the Europeans arrived – hunting, fishing and foraging while also cultivating corn, beans and squash. They called the island centre Mannahatta, or 'the place where we get bows', a nod to its plentiful timber supply. Among the natural resources on which the Lenape relied were beavers, soon coveted by the Dutch settlers, too. Tragically, the spread of smallpox and other European diseases killed countless Lenape. As legend goes, the fate-sealing exchange came in the form of a simple sale: Dutch governor Peter Minuit formally purchased Manhattan from the Native Americans on 24 May 1626 in what is now Inwood Hill Park, at the northern tip of the island. The price? Trinkets valued at $24. Relationships quickly deteriorated. Beginning in 1641, the colonists and the Lenape warred against one another, in part due to savage leadership by New Netherland Director William Kieft. By the century's end, the Lenape had largely vanished from their homeland.

3-SECOND SURVEY
Early New Yorkers – Lenape and Dutch alike – were as passionate about their hometown as today's denizens. Unfortunately, they didn't feel the same about each other.

3-MINUTE OVERVIEW
Although the colonists initially relied on the Lenape for friendship and trade, once they became self-sufficient, relations quickly declined and conflicts ensued. On 25 February 1643, against the wishes of many Dutch settlers, Director Kieft led a raid against a Lenape group, murdering more than 100 unarmed men, women and children. Following the massacre, Dutchman David Pietersz de Vries, an opponent of Kieft, met with chief Penhawitz to broker peace, but any resolution was fleeting.

RELATED ENTRY
See also
THE CITY TAKES SHAPE
page 14

3-SECOND BIOGRAPHIES
DAVID PIETERSZ DE VRIES
c.1593–1655
Dutch patroon who met with Lenape chief Penhawitz on 4 March 1643, regarding deteriorating relations between the two groups

PETER MINUIT
1580–1638
Director of New Netherland, who purchased the island of Manhattan from the Lenape

PENHAWITZ
fl c.1640
Lenape leader well known in New Amsterdam, who represented the Canarsee branch of his people

30-SECOND TEXT
Jennifer Shalant

Henry Hudson left Amsterdam in search of a passage to China with a crew of 18 and funds from the Dutch East India Company.

Hudſons·Riuer

THE ENGLISH

the 30-second tour

In 1664, when an English fleet
sailed through the Narrows to take possession
of the Dutch city of New Netherland, only a
very small number of English families lived in
Manhattan. Most of the residents of the newly
rechristened city of New York were Dutch-
speaking French, German, Scandinavian and
Dutch Protestants. Although the English
remained a minority, Englishmen dominated
the high political offices and prominent
occupations. Trinity Church, the first parish
of the Church of England in New York, was
formed in 1697 and quickly became the leading
congregation in the city. English families that
had been worshipping in the Dutch Reformed
Church returned to the Anglican fold, and many
Dutchmen changed their allegiances, furthering
the Anglicization of the leading families.
As Dutch vernacular gave way to English,
Lower Manhattan's old streets names were
overwritten, and Broadway, Wall, Beaver and
Pearl streets entered the lexicon. English
newspapers and religious denominations such
as Quaker, Baptist and Presbyterian furthered
English influence, and immigration from the
whole of the British Isles cemented English
dominance of social and commercial life. By
the time of the American Revolution, New York
was the third-largest city in the British Empire.

3-SECOND SURVEY
The English gave New
York its name, its oldest
park and the best-endowed
parish church in the
United States.

3-MINUTE OVERVIEW
The English have not
disappeared from New
York: St. George's Society
– founded in 1770 by
Englishmen for the relief
of their countrymen who
had fallen on hard times
or were in distress –
remains the city's leading
English charity. As well
as providing financial
help for both the elderly
and the disabled, St
George's also funds
scholarships for students
academically gifted.

RELATED ENTRIES
See also
WELCOME TO NEW YORK
page 42

THE IRISH
page 44

3-SECOND BIOGRAPHY
EDWARD HYDE,
LORD CORNBURY
1661–1723
Governor of New York,
1701–08, widely thought to
be corrupt. A purported
portrait at the New York
Historical Society depicts him
in the full woman's clothing
he was accused of wearing.

30-SECOND TEXT
Andrew Kryzak

*At the start of the
American Revolution,
English New Yorkers
were the city's
dominant ethnic
group in terms of both
numbers and influence.*

11 January 1755
Born on the British island of Nevis in the West Indies to Rachel Faucett, who was not married to his father

1765
Moves to St. Croix; abandoned by his father

1768
Hamilton's mother dies of yellow fever; he nearly dies as well

1772
A hurricane ravages the Virgin Islands; Hamilton's sponsors fund his passage abroad

1775
Joins a New York militia to fight the British

1777
Appointed lieutenant colonel on George Washington's staff

1782
Elected to the Continental Congress

1784
Helps found the Bank of New York

1788
Leads the fight for New York to ratify the United States Constitution

1789
Appointed first secretary of the Treasury as George Washington is elected first president

1801
Advises federalists to back Thomas Jefferson over Aaron Burr in deadlocked election

11 July 1804
Loses duel against Vice-President Aaron Burr in New Jersey

12 July 1804
Dies at a friend's home in Greenwich Village

ALEXANDER HAMILTON

In April 2009, the White House invited New York City composer Lin-Manuel Miranda to participate in an evening of music and poetry reflecting 'the American Experience'. Rather than contribute a song from *In the Heights* – his 2008 Tony Award-winning musical about Dominican Americans in Manhattan – Miranda surprised his hosts with a captivating rap about the nation's first Secretary of the Treasury: Alexander Hamilton.

Six years later, *Hamilton* premiered on Broadway. If its rapturous reviews are not enough to convince you that a hip-hop musical about the man who wrote 51 of the 85 *Federalist* papers makes perfect sense, try this: visualize Thomas Jefferson, George Washington or James Madison at home on their vast Virginia plantations. Now picture Hamilton, their contemporary, in his notoriously colourful clothes on the streets of his teeming city. A New Yorker by choice not birth, Hamilton loathed country life as thoroughly as Jefferson despised cities. Jefferson mistrusted banks and money; Hamilton considered commerce the lifeblood of the new nation. The fact that Hamilton was born elsewhere – impoverished, out of wedlock, on the small Caribbean island of Nevis in 1755 – only made him more of a New Yorker: this is a city in which 37 per cent of the current population was born in another country. Hamilton is their patron saint, incarnating that most American of identities: the immigrant striver – industrious, brash, brilliant.

Hamilton sailed to New York after a 1772 hurricane devastated the Virgin Islands. He never looked back, attending King's (now Columbia) College; founding the world's first voter-based political party and the *New York Post*; establishing a national bank and budget system; donating his legal services to African Americans kidnapped from city streets and sold back into slavery. His impulses were not all so industrious: Hamilton also had a starring role in the nation's first political sex scandal and was dead at 49 – killed in a duel by Vice-President Aaron Burr.

Sarah Fenton

AFRICAN AMERICANS IN NEW YORK

the 30-second tour

3-SECOND SURVEY
In the city of contradictions, energetic civil rights movements have existed alongside entrenched racism for much of New York's history.

3-MINUTE OVERVIEW
Even with segregation illegal, discrimination plagued the city's public-school system during the civil rights era. Schools in Harlem, Bedford-Stuyvesant and other predominantly non-white neighbourhoods were overcrowded and underserved. Despite protests for integration – and a citywide boycott by more than 400,000 children in February 1964 – school segregation persisted in the civil rights era and continues to a lesser extent today. In 2015, City Council passed the School Diversity Accountability Act to help combat this issue.

Far above the 'Mason-Dixon line' that connotes the divide between the liberal North and conservative South, New York has had a troubled history of race relations. The first enslaved Africans came to New Amsterdam in 1625, and slavery persisted for two centuries until it was finally abolished in New York in 1827. But many New Yorkers continued to defend slavery, and tensions erupted in July 1863 with the Draft Riots, an episode of mob violence targeting local African Americans and abolitionists during the Civil War. After the war, though bigotry remained a formidable obstacle, the city nurtured a new generation of activists, giving rise to the National Association for the Advancement of Colored People (NAACP) in 1909, and offering economic opportunities for African Americans migrating out of the South. By the 1920s, the Harlem Renaissance took hold, with the neighbourhood attracting black writers, artists and musicians such as Langston Hughes, Ella Fitzgerald and Zora Neale Hurston, who reshaped the city's social and cultural landscape and captured the world's attention. During the post-war civil rights era, with racial segregation festering in city businesses and schools, African-American New Yorkers and their allies mobilized against discriminatory policies – and ignited reforms nationwide.

RELATED ENTRIES
See also
PROTEST!
page 62

HARLEM RENAISSANCE
page 124

3-SECOND BIOGRAPHIES
DAVID RUGGLES
1810–49
African-American abolitionist, secretary of the New York Committee of Vigilance, housed a 'station' on New York's Underground Railroad and helped nearly 600 escaped slaves

ADAM CLAYTON POWELL JR.
1908–72
Civil rights activist and first African American New Yorker elected to Congress

30-SECOND TEXT
Jennifer Shalant

Center of abolitionism, hotbed of artistic activity, crucible of protest and reform – New York City plays a starring role in the story of black America.

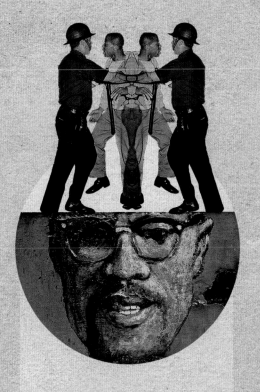

WELCOME
TO
HARLEM USA

WELCOME TO NEW YORK

the 30-second tour

'Give me your tired, your poor, your huddled masses yearning to breathe free.' Such are the words attributed to the Statue of Liberty, that 'Mother of Exiles' standing 93m (305ft) above Liberty Island in New York Harbour, offering 'world-wide welcome' to weary travellers from the torch in her exultantly raised right hand. The warmth of that welcome has waxed and waned in a country that both celebrates and spasmodically forgets it is a nation of immigrants. In her shadow sits the federal immigration centre at Ellis Island, where more than 12 million pilgrims entered the country between opening day on 1 January 1892, and its official closure in November 1954. During its peak from 1900 to 1914, up to 10,000 hopefuls passed daily through the Great Hall, pausing to be examined by inspectors who could deny entry on a variety of grounds – from contagious disease to anarchist sympathies or 'low moral character'; only about 2 per cent were in fact turned back. After exchanging their remaining gold or currency and retrieving luggage they'd left home with weeks, months or even years before, these new Americans set out for the future, whether by ferry to Manhattan or by trains further north, south or west. Four in ten Americans are estimated to have an ancestor who came through Ellis Island.

3-SECOND SURVEY
The nation's most populous city, New York remains the leading gateway for immigrants entering the country legally, and Lady Liberty her city's most visited site.

3-MINUTE OVERVIEW
In a city as raucously democratic as New York, the meanings of public memorials are never merely handed down by their designers but creatively reimagined by citizens over time. Intended to affiliate Republican France with a triumphant Union government, the Statue of Liberty has instead become – since her lavish unveiling in October 1886 – a testament to immigration in a city with more than 3 million foreign-born inhabitants, more than any other city in the world.

RELATED ENTRIES
See also
THE IRISH
page 44

PUBLIC HEALTH
page 94

3-SECOND BIOGRAPHIES
FRÉDÉRIC AUGUSTE BARTHOLDI
1834–1904
French sculptor who designed the Statue of Liberty

ANNIE MOORE
1874–1924
The first immigrant to come through Ellis Island, travelling from County Cork, Ireland, aboard the steamship *Nevada* with her two younger brothers

30-SECOND TEXT
Sarah Fenton

Never intended as a 'gift' from France, Lady Liberty was paid for in stops and starts by a first resentful – but finally affectionate – public.

THE IRISH

the 30-second tour

The Irish immigrants of the

eighteenth century fled to America to escape England's restrictive Penal Laws, following trade routes that transported flaxseed to New York City; too destitute to go further, most settled there. The largest wave of immigration occurred in 1846–55 in the wake of the Great Famine that devastated Ireland's potato crops. Facilitated by a shared language, long-established trade ties and chain immigration, 2 million of Ireland's mostly Roman Catholic citizens boarded 'coffin ships' for New York. Burdened by a history of poverty, religious persecution and discrimination, they performed unskilled jobs for low pay and crammed into tenements in the notorious Five Points slums. Through their close association with the Democratic Party organization Tammany Hall, the Irish became a powerful political group; immigrants showed their appreciation at the polls for food baskets and 'legal aid' provided by the party. Famous for extorting voters, Tammany Hall later became synonymous with political corruption: driving Democratic Party nominations, electing officials and influencing policymaking. Today the Irish continue to play a significant role in the city's police, fire and sanitation departments, local and state politics, the Roman Catholic Church and the popular St Patrick's Day Parade.

3-SECOND SURVEY
The Irish are among New York's most prominent ethnic groups, and at one point there were more Irish in New York than in Dublin.

3-MINUTE OVERVIEW
Despite their harsh welcome, Irish immigrants were crucial to the city's growth: men laboured in the gangs that built the Erie Canal, Central and Prospect parks, the subway tunnels and the Brooklyn Bridge. Women worked as domestic servants, laundresses and – during the boom of the garment industry – seamstresses, playing their part in one of the few immigrant groups in which women outnumbered men.

RELATED ENTRIES
See also
ETHNIC VILLAGES ON THE LOWER EAST SIDE
page 46

GANGS OF NEW YORK
page 96

3-SECOND BIOGRAPHIES
WILLIAM MAGEAR 'BOSS' TWEED
1823–78
American real-estate tycoon, Tammany Hall leader infamous for embezzling millions in New York tax dollars

WILLIAM RUSSELL GRACE
1832–1904
Shipping entrepreneur and the first Irish-Catholic Mayor of New York

30-SECOND TEXT
Cheong Kim

There are more Irish-Americans in New York than in any other American city, playing significant roles in the city's Catholic churches, police and fire departments.

ETHNIC VILLAGES ON THE LOWER EAST SIDE

the 30-second tour

At the turn of the twentieth

century, 1.4 million Jews fled the pogroms of eastern Europe and clustered on Manhattan's Lower East Side in overstuffed tenements festering with crime and disease. Many sewed garments for pennies per piece. Finally free to practise their faith and language, they opened mikvahs, yeshivas and kosher marts. Yiddish theatre and newspapers thrived. By 1910, 10,000 Italians had settled in neighbouring Little Italy. Destitute after the unification of their country, they organized themselves according to their home villages, worked in the city's municipal sector and processed down Mulberry Street to celebrate funerals and christenings. In 1921 the Immigration Act restricted new arrivals; those able to escape the slums moved to other parts of the city. In 1965 the Chinese arrived in earnest along Little Italy's southern border. Buoyed by a steady stream of Asian immigrants, Chinatown continues to expand, repurposing synagogues as Buddhist temples and once Jewish- and Italian-owned businesses as Chinese restaurants and grocers. Today, few vestiges of Jewish immigrant life remain; a smattering of pasta joints and the San Gennaro festival pass for Italian culture. Nonetheless, the Lower East Side remains a popular destination for those wanting a taste of New York's immigrant communities.

3-SECOND SURVEY
In a city of immigrants, Manhattan's Lower East Side has long been a gateway for their arrival.

3-MINUTE OVERVIEW
Jews, Italians and Chinese, fleeing religious persecution and poverty, arrived in New York to find themselves exploited in dangerous, low-paying jobs and – unfamiliar with the culture and language – victims of bigotry and exclusion. Denied access to businesses and services, they created insular towns complete with their own languages, customs and financial and cultural institutions – communities shaped as much by discrimination as by ethnic and cultural pride.

RELATED ENTRIES
See also
WELCOME TO NEW YORK
page 42

GANGS OF NEW YORK
page 96

3-SECOND BIOGRAPHIES
VINCENZO SELLARO
1868–1932
Gynaecologist and founder of the Order of the Sons of Italy in America, to help new Italian immigrants settle in New York

LEE LOK
1869–1942
Proprietor of Quong Yuen Shing & Company, oldest shop in Chinatown

RUTH J. ABRAM
1946–
Historian, social activist and founder of the Lower East Side Tenement Museum

30-SECOND TEXT
Cheong Kim

Known as much for its radical politics as its spicy food, the Lower East Side's streets, papers and playhouses have long nurtured transnational debate.

GOVERNING THE LAND

Anti-federalist In the aftermath of the American Revolution, an opponent of stronger federal government.

Bedford-Stuyvesant Neighbourhood in north-central Brooklyn that from the 1920s onwards was, after Harlem, the city's main centre for its African-American population. Nicknamed 'Bed-Stuy', the area has a large number of now highly coveted brownstones. Brooklyn-raised movie director Spike Lee's 1989 hit *Do the Right Thing* dramatized an overspill of racial tensions on a hot summer's day in Bed-Stuy.

Big Board The nickname for the New York Stock Exchange at 11 Wall Street, Lower Manhattan.

The draft Conscription to the armed forces, which was imposed in the United States Civil War, the First World War, the Second World War, the Korean War and the Vietnam War.

Dylan Thomas Welsh poet who was staying at the Chelsea Hotel in Greenwich Village while in the United States for a poetry-reading tour when he fell ill after prolonged heavy drinking and died in St Vincent's Hospital on 9 November 1953. His poem *Do Not Go Gentle Into That Good Night* was published in *In Country Sleep and Other Poems* (1952).

Emancipation Proclamation Executive order and proclamation issued by President Lincoln on 1 January 1863, which declared more than 3 million slaves in specific areas of the South to be free. It made the abolition of slavery an explicit aim of the Union in the United States Civil War against the Confederacy in the South.

Homeland Security Act United States legislation (2002) introduced in response to the 9/11 attacks. It created a new Department of Homeland Security and Secretary of Homeland Security.

NASDAQ Stock exchange at 1 Liberty Plaza, 165 Broadway in Manhattan; the world's second largest stock exchange after the New York Stock Exchange. The initials stand for the National Association of Securities Dealers Automated Quotations. It was founded in 1971.

Son of Sam Serial killer, real name David Berkowitz, who killed six and wounded seven in 1976–77 mostly using a .44 caliber Bulldog revolver. He was captured by the NYPD in August 1977, confessed and was sentenced to 25 years to life for each of the killings.

Stamp Act Controversial revenue-raising British legislation of 1765 that required printed papers such as legal documents and newspapers in the British colonies of America to use stamped paper on which a tax was payable.

Turtle Bay Neighbourhood on the eastern edge of Midtown Manhattan to the east of Lexington Avenue, and home to the Chrysler Building as well as the United Nations Headquarters. Turtle Bay's Tudor City apartments, built 1927–32, stand on the site of the celebrated 'Corcoran's Roost', an Irish shanty town known for violent crime and gang activity. Also in the neighbourhood is Turtle Bay Gardens, a redeveloped area of brownstones with communal gardens, which has been home to celebrities including Katharine Hepburn, Stephen Sondheim and Leopold Stokowski. Children's author E. B. White wrote *Charlotte's Web* there.

Wall Street Crash Stock-market crash at the New York Stock Exchange that began on Thursday 24 October 1929 and reached its peak on the following Tuesday, 29 October, when the market lost $14 billion. The crash ushered in the Great Depression that lasted until the late 1930s.

War on Terror United States-led international military campaign from 2001 onwards against terrorist organizations and states that harbour or support them. President George W. Bush first used the phrase on 20 September, 2001, in the wake of the 9/11 attacks.

World Trade Center Complex of seven buildings in Lower Manhattan opened in 1973 as part of an urban regeneration project. Its twin towers – 1 and 2 World Trade Center (otherwise known as the North and South towers) were at the time the world's tallest buildings at 417 m (1,368 ft) and 415 m (1,362 ft) respectively. Both collapsed when aircraft were flown into them in the 9/11 attacks. The new One World Trade Center skyscraper (also 417 m/1,368 ft at roof height), was built alongside memorials and opened in 2013.

GLOBAL CITY

the 30-second tour

3-SECOND SURVEY
Economics alone do not a global city make: New York adds renowned cultural institutions, major media outlets, mass transit networks and a breathtakingly diverse population.

3-MINUTE OVERVIEW
It seems only fitting that the United Nations – an international organization whose member states have endeavoured to promote global peace and economic development since the end of the Second World War – would be headquartered in a city with 800 spoken languages. The UN's grounds, which include the imposing Secretariat Building and General Assembly Hall and border the East River in Manhattan's Turtle Bay, are considered International Territory and are not bound by Unites States law.

The Dutch East India Company was the first to issue stocks and bonds. It was also sponsor to Sir Henry Hudson, who in 1609 sailed into what is now New York City in search of a faster trade route to China. Instead, he was met by a 'new' world, rich in natural abundance. With the arrival of Dutch settlers came transatlantic disease and the transformation of that abundant landscape into marketable commodities. By 1613, the Dutch had established a trading post on the western edge of Manhattan, near land that would one day see the rise and fall of the World Trade Center. Natural harbours encouraged international shipping, and extant barriers to trade and immigration diminished over the eighteenth and nineteenth centuries. New York City has stood at the centre of world finance since the Second World War and is currently home to the world's largest central business district and two largest stock exchanges (the New York Stock Exchange and NASDAQ). As ever, globalism has its costs: the 2008 financial crisis destabilized markets an ocean away. Henry Hudson sailed that ocean more than four centuries ago to facilitate Dutch trade with China; the city he encountered instead now calls China its leading growth market for exports, and is home to the largest Chinese population outside China.

RELATED ENTRIES
See also
WELCOME TO NEW YORK
page 42

NYSE & AMEX:
GROWTH & CRASHES
page 54

3-SECOND BIOGRAPHIES
SASKIA SASSEN
1947–
Dutch-American professor of sociology at Columbia University who coined the term 'global city'

TIMOTHY GEITHNER
1961–
New York City-born banker who served as secretary of the United States Treasury in 2009–13 in the aftermath of the global financial crisis

30-SECOND TEXT
Sarah Fenton

The most significant nodes in the global marketplace, London and New York remain more integrated with the worldwide economy than any other cities.

NYSE & AMEX: GROWTH & CRASHES

the 30-second tour

On 17 May 1792, a group of stockbrokers met under a buttonwood tree on Wall Street to formalize trading arrangements and commissions, out of which agreement the New York Stock Exchange (NYSE) was organized. Brokers without the capital to trade on the NYSE met their clients on the curb and traded in younger and riskier stocks. These brokers also organized, formulated trading rules and in 1953 became known as the American Stock Exchange. New York's securities exchanges have long been at the centre of American capitalism, and their growth has mirrored that of the American economy as a whole. The exchanges provided the means of securing the capital that financed the expansion of American industry across the continent. They also fuelled periods of intense speculation that led to repeated panics, market crashes and depressions throughout the nineteenth and early twentieth centuries. These were only a prequel to the Wall Street Crash of 1929, which set off the Great Depression. The symbolic power of the NYSE as the anchor of Wall Street is long established. When in 1920 a bomb was set off on Wall Street, it was detonated at the corner of Wall and Broad streets, diagonally opposite the Big Board.

RELATED ENTRY
See also
GLOBAL CITY
page 52

3-SECOND BIOGRAPHY
J.P. MORGAN
1837–1913
Practitioner of high finance, whose banking house refinanced and restructured the Erie Canal and the New York Central railroads as well as General Electric, AT&T and US Steel

30-SECOND TEXT
Andrew Kryzak

Love it or loathe it – Wall Street is both shorthand for the financial markets of the entire country and a symbol of this specific city.

THE MAYORS

the 30-second tour

The mayor is chief executive of New York City. He – and to date all have been men – runs the largest municipal government in the United States. He is responsible for more than 300,000 employees, the largest police force in the country (34,500 officers) and the largest school system (1 million students). He dominates the budget process ($79 billion), and – through the department of city planning and his appointment of the chair of the city planning commission – dominates land-use decisions as well. He controls more than 60 agencies that affect virtually every aspect of urban life: the building code and pothole repair, environmental safety and public health, city-sponsored cultural events and parks, economic development programmes, and the administration of social welfare services. Eligible citizens vote for the mayor in citywide elections for four-year terms. Although registered Democrats have a huge majority in New York City, for 43 of the past 82 years voters have chosen mayors from other parties. The mayor is also the ceremonial leader of New York City and typically the country's best-known elected official nationally and internationally after the president of the United States. New York's mayor is unusually powerful by United States standards, sharing authority with a relatively weak city council.

3-SECOND SURVEY
One mayor described his role this way: 'If a sparrow dies of a heart attack in Central Park, the people hold me responsible.'

3-MINUTE OVERVIEW
Many New York City mayors have been colourful characters: Fiorello La Guardia (1934–45) read comic strips over the radio during a newspaper strike; Edward I. Koch (1978–89) cheered pedestrians walking over the Brooklyn Bridge during a transit strike; Rudolph Giuliani (1994–2001) became an international hero who was awarded the Order of the British Empire for his response to the 9/11 terror attack; Michael Bloomberg (2002–13) was the richest man in New York City.

RELATED ENTRIES
See also
NYPD BLUES
page 58

URBAN PLANNING
page 82

3-SECOND BIOGRAPHIES
ROBERT F. WAGNER JR.
1910–91
One of only four mayors to serve three terms, 1954–65

DAVID DINKINS
1927–
The city's only African-American mayor to date

BILL DE BLASIO
1961–
New York's 109th mayor, who began his term on 1 January 2014

30-SECOND TEXT
Chris McNickle

Built in 1812, New York City Hall is the oldest city hall in the United States to still house its original governmental functions, including the Mayor's office.

NYPD BLUES

the 30-second tour

During the sweltering summer of 1977, New York City serial killer 'Son of Sam' murdered six people and eluded capture while taunting the police and achieving worldwide notoriety. July of that summer saw a citywide blackout enable arson and looting. On 26 February 1988, NYPD officer Edward Byrne was shot on a Queens street corner at the behest of drug dealers in a year that endured 1,896 homicides. Each incident was a symbol of the lawlessness that characterized the city in decades when entire neighbourhoods felt bombed out – deserts of drugs and muggings, abandoned buildings and defaced surfaces. New York is now the safest major city in the United States, and 2014 saw a record low 328 homicides. What changed? It depends who you ask. In 1994, newly inaugurated mayor Rudy Giuliani appointed police commissioner Bill Bratton to implement 'stop-and-frisk' and 'broken-windows'. These methods of policing were premised on the theory that serious crime can be averted by cracking down on nuisance offences, from turnstile-jumping to panhandling, public intoxication and drug possession. These are also methods that disproportionately target minorities (one in 15 African-American men are jailed compared to 1 in every 106 white men) and yield mass incarceration.

RELATED ENTRIES
See also
THE MAYORS
page 58

PROTEST!
page 62

PUBLIC HEALTH
page 94

3-SECOND SURVEY
Singular as the 1970s felt, every city witnesses cycles of lawlessness followed by order, often imposed at great cost to some part of its citizenry.

3-MINUTE OVERVIEW
New York City's policing has evolved from night-time 'foot patrols' in New Amsterdam (eight men armed with rattles) to a paid force of 36 men in 1741 (only 12 of them on duty at any given time) to the 1845 establishment of the NYPD. It now maintains the nation's largest municipal police force. It consumes 15 per cent of the city's annual budget and employs more people than the FBI, including 34,500 uniformed officers – or roughly four cops per 1,000 people.

3-SECOND BIOGRAPHIES
THOMAS F. BYRNES
1842–1910
Irish-born NYPD captain whose tough suspect interrogations popularized the term 'the third degree'

FRANK SERPICO
1936–
Brooklyn-born Italian-American NYPD officer and whistle-blower who prompted Mayor John Lindsay to establish the 1970 Knapp Commission to confirm police corruption

30-SECOND TEXT
Sarah Fenton

In 1845, a paid professional police force replaced the civilian militia for the first time in New York City's history.

30 November 1924
Born in Brooklyn to a
Barbadian mother and
Guyanese father

1959–64
Educational consultant in
the day-care division of
the New York City Bureau
of Child Welfare

1964
Elected to the New York
State Assembly as a
Democrat from Bushwick
and Bedford-Stuyvesant

1968
Becomes the first black
woman elected to the
United States House
of Representatives

1970
Publishes autobiography
Unbought and Unbossed

1972
Runs for president as the
first African American –
and the first woman – to
seek nomination by a
major political party,
declaring: 'I am the
candidate of the people.'

1973
Publishes *The Good Fight*

1982
Leaves Washington, DC,
after serving seven
terms in the House
of Representatives

1983–87
Holds the Purington Chair
at Mount Holyoke
College, South Hadley,
Massachusetts

1 January 2005
Dies in Ormond
Beach, Florida

2015
Posthumously awarded
the Presidential Medal
of Freedom

SHIRLEY CHISHOLM

Traditionally, committee

assignments in the United States House of Representatives are made by seniority, with newcomers expected to serve deferentially wherever they are assigned. Shirley Chisholm wasn't having it. Elected in 1968 to represent New York's 12th Congressional District – then an exceptionally dense slice of Bedford-Stuyvesant with nary a farm to be found – she was assigned to the House Agricultural Committee. Chisholm was furious, believing the party elders who made the assignment to be either hostile to her or indifferent to her constituency. But in a style that defined a lifetime of public service, Chisholm turned her own fury into a fight on behalf of those she had sworn to represent, using the Committee to channel surplus food to hungry New Yorkers, expanding the food-stamp programme and helping create the Special Supplemental Nutrition Program for Women, Infants and Children (WIC). Chisholm summarized her governing philosophy succinctly: 'Service is the rent that you pay for room on this earth.'

This was not her first fight: 'Mother always said that even when I was three, I used to get the six- and seven-year-old kids on the block and punch them and say, "Listen to me."' Born in Brooklyn to immigrant parents, Chisholm spent part of her girlhood with a grandmother in Barbados. She returned to New York in 1934 and went on to become a debate champ at Brooklyn College. As much as she loved a good fight, Chisholm wanted to fight for good, and working on behalf of children became her calling. While earning a master's degree in elementary education at Columbia University, Chisholm also taught at nursery school in Brooklyn and Lower Manhattan, winning widespread recognition as an authority on early education and child welfare.

By the 1960s, the children of Chisholm's beloved Bed-Stuy were struggling; infant-mortality rates were twice the city average and high-school drop-out rates approached 70 per cent. But the 1960 census had segregated the neighbourhood into five districts, each with a white representative who evinced little understanding of the neighbourhood's actual needs. The 1964 Civil Rights Act required that map be redrawn, and four years later Chisholm became the first black woman to serve in Congress, explaining simply 'the people wanted me'. In 1972 Chisholm became the first African American and the first woman to mount a serious campaign for the presidency, receiving 151 delegates and laying the groundwork for the diverse candidates of the twenty-first century.

Sarah Fenton

PROTEST!

the 30-second tour

New Yorkers seldom shy from a fight – particularly one waged noisily and in public. Mobs paraded through Manhattan with effigies of elected officials to protest the Stamp Act in 1765 – 'No taxation without representation!' Triumph in the American Revolution did not bring peace to the streets: anti-federalist Thomas Greenleaf saw his printing office razed in 1788 by supporters of the newly proposed United States constitution. The bloodiest riots in American history tore through Manhattan on 13–17 July 1863, just months after President Lincoln issued the Emancipation Proclamation. What began as resistance to the first federal conscription act became an assault on black New Yorkers by crowds of mostly Irish labourers. Early twentieth-century protests arose most often from labour unrest. Strikers demanded an end to the 60-hour working week and treacherous conditions that made possible such tragedies as the Triangle Shirtwaist fire (which killed 146 workers). Anger at the draft fuelled protests in the 1960s as it had a century before: Columbia University students opposed to the War in Vietnam cheered as their spring classes were cancelled in 1968 amidst spirited rallies and the occupation of campus buildings.

RELATED ENTRIES
See also
NYPD BLUES
page 58

COUNTERCULTURAL
NEW YORK
page 108

3-SECOND SURVEY
By 1960, nearly 90 per cent of American households had televisions, bringing protests off the streets and into the living rooms of even the meekest New Yorkers.

3-MINUTE OVERVIEW
From 2016 presidential hopeful Bernie Sanders' pledge to 'wage a moral and political war against the billionaires and corporate leaders on Wall Street', to his primary opponent (and former New York Senator) Hillary Clinton's pointed insistence that 'black lives do *indeed* matter' – New York City's biggest protest movements of the twenty-first century have resonated far beyond the days when they had boots on the ground, whether camping in Zuccotti Park or marching down Fifth Avenue.

3-SECOND BIOGRAPHIES
SAMUEL GOMPERS
1850–1924
Founder of the American Federation of Labor in 1886 to fight on behalf of shorter hours and higher wages

MALCOLM X
1925–65
Unapologetic protestor who gained national attention in 1957 for confronting the NYPD officers responsible for beating fellow Nation of Islam member Johnson Hinton

30-SECOND TEXT
Sarah Fenton

In keeping with the idea 'all politics is local', many of New York's protest movements were homegrown; others, such as women's suffrage, were international.

9/11

the 30-second tour

At 8.45 a.m on 11 September 2001, a Boeing 767 cut through the clear blue sky over New York City and exploded into the North Tower of the World Trade Center. Initial assumptions of a freak accident were dispelled 18 minutes later when a second plane sliced through its 'twin' South Tower. Within an hour and a half, both 110-storey skyscrapers had collapsed, showering debris, enflaming neighbouring buildings and sending shocked, dust-covered New Yorkers stumbling into the streets. The Twin Towers' collapse was part of four coordinated acts of terrorism in which 19 militants associated with the Islamic extremist group al-Qaeda hijacked commercial airplanes and – in retaliation for United States involvement in the Middle East – plummeted them in suicide attacks onto prominent national landmarks. A third plane hit the Pentagon in Arlington County, Virginia. A fourth, headed for Washington, D.C., crash-landed near Shanksville, Pennsylvania. The attacks had wide-reaching effects – halting trading on Wall Street, disrupting civilian airspace and transportation, and requiring the evacuation of more than 1 million workers and residents of lower Manhattan. In May 2011, after evading capture for nearly a decade, al-Qaeda leader Osama bin Laden was killed by a Special Forces unit of the United States military.

3-SECOND SURVEY
The attacks of 9/11 killed nearly 3,000 people and injured 6,000 more in what is regarded as the most devastating terrorist attack in American history.

3-MINUTE OVERVIEW
The Twin Towers were among seven buildings that comprised the World Trade Center, a complex that housed 430 companies from 28 countries. Following the attack, the Center was rebuilt to include a grove of white oak trees, a memorial museum and, in the towers' footprints, twin pools – the largest man-made waterfalls in the United States – whose parapets are etched with the victims' names, 343 of whom were New York City firefighters.

RELATED ENTRIES
See also
NYSE & AMEX:
GROWTH & CRASHES
page 54

NYPD BLUES
page 58

3-SECOND BIOGRAPHIES
RUDOLPH WILLIAM LOUIS 'RUDY' GIULIANI
1944–
Mayor of New York City during the 9/11 attacks who was widely praised – earning him the title 'America's Mayor'

CYRIL RICHARD 'RICK' RESCORLA
1939–2001
Director of security for Morgan Stanley in the World Trade Center, credited with saving more than 2,600 lives; died during rescue

30-SECOND TEXT
Cheong Kim

The impact of 9/11 is present still in the bonds between citizens, the worldwide carnage, and the continued struggles of the heroic first responders.

IMPROVING THE LAND

Beaux Arts Neoclassical architectural style, originally French and highly popular in New York and the United States in 1880–1920.

Brooklyn Dodgers Baseball team founded, as the Brooklyn Grays, in 1883. In honour of locals' ability to navigate the streets without being hit by speeding trolley cars, they were nicknamed the Brooklyn Trolley Dodgers in 1895 – soon afterwards shortened to 'the Dodgers'. They played at three Brooklyn stadiums before settling at Ebbets Fields in Flatbush in 1913. They had a major rivalry with the New York Giants, which continued after both teams moved to California in 1957, the Dodgers to LA and the Giants to San Francisco.

Chrysler Building Midtown landmark, a 319 m (1,046 ft)-tall skyscraper designed by Brooklyn-born architect William Van Alen. The Chrysler, which opened in 1930 at 42nd Street and Lexington Avenue, is an Art Deco masterpiece: it has corner ornamentation on the 31st floor that replicates the radiator caps on the 1929 Chrysler motor car and an exquisite seven-arch terraced crown.

Cross Bronx Expressway Freeway built in 1948–72 under city planner Robert Moses. Its construction was blamed for exacerbating urban decay in South Bronx neighbourhoods and problems associated with it fuelled forthright opposition to other urban expressways.

Empire State Building One of the New York icons, this Art Deco-style, 102-storey, 443 m (1,454 ft)-tall skyscraper on Fifth Avenue was completed in 1931 and was the tallest building in the world until the completion of the North Tower of the World Trade Center in 1970. It was designed by architects Shreve, Lamb and Harmon.

Grand Central Terminal Landmark rail station in Midtown, built 1903–13 to replace the earlier station on the site. Two firms of architects cooperated on the design: Reed & Stern (a firm from St Paul, Minnesota) handled the overall station design, while New York firm Warren & Wetmore (designers of the New York Yacht Club) oversaw architectural detail, notably the fine Beaux Arts styling.

'I have a bridge to sell you' Phrase associated with American con man George C Parker (1870–1936), who was notorious for attempting to sell public buildings and structures to gullible folk – including, more than once, the Brooklyn Bridge. He claimed to be able to sell the potentially lucrative control over access to the bridge. Other structures he tried to sell included the Statue of Liberty and General Grant's Tomb in Morningside Heights. After his third conviction for fraud, in 1928, he was sentenced to life imprisonment.

Lincoln Center Performing-arts centre in the Lincoln Square neighbourhood of Manhattan, built 1955–69. Its first venue, Philharmonic Hall, opened in 1962. The New York City Ballet, the New York Philharmonic and the Metropolitan Opera all perform there.

One57 Nicknamed 'the Billionaire Building', another of Manhattan's super-tall skyscrapers, this one standing 306 m (1,004 ft) to its roof at 157 West 57th Street in Midtown. It contains 92 condominiums on top of a 210-room Park Hyatt hotel.

Pennsylvania Station Rail terminal in Midtown, popularly known as Penn Station. The ornate original building (1901–10) was demolished in 1963 and the modern terminal was constructed. It is underground, beneath Madison Square Garden and between Seventh and Eighth Avenue.

Progressive Era Period of political reform and social change in the 1890s–1920s.

The Bowery Lower Manhattan street and neighbourhood. The name comes from Dutch bouwerij ('farm') because this southern area of the island was once agricultural land. The street runs from Chatham Square in Chinatown to Cooper Square.

West Side Elevated Highway Elevated roadway in Manhattan alongside the Hudson River, built 1929–51. The West Side Highway quickly deteriorated and was closed in 1973 after a collapse led to a car and truck falling through it at 14th Street.

Woolworth Building Neo-Gothic early New York skyscraper designed by Cass Gilbert at 233 Broadway in Manhattan, and opened in 1913. It stands 241.4 m (792 ft) tall and was the tallest building in the world from 1913 to 1930.

WATERWAYS

the 30-second tour

New York is a port city. In the middle of the 19th century, 75 per cent of all customs revenue for the United States was collected in the port of New York; the port of New York and New Jersey remains the busiest on the East Coast of the United States. All of this has been made possible by New York's enviable situation at the head of one of the world's greatest natural harbours. The saline waters of New York Harbor, which sits at the confluence of a complex system of tidal estuaries, almost never freeze and have thus provided a year-round home to waterborne commerce for hundreds of years. In 1825, when the Erie Canal opened the only all-water route from the Great Lakes to the Atlantic Ocean via New York Harbor, New York instantly became the most important mercantile centre in the United States. Its waterways include not only the harbour itself, but the two large estuaries of the Hudson River and the East River. Both have long served as commercial routes for shipping as well as commuter arteries for the ferries that have plied the harbour since the Dutch made the first organized river crossing in 1642.

RELATED ENTRY
See also
BRIDGES & TUNNELS
page 78

3-SECOND BIOGRAPHIES
HENRY HUDSON
died 1611
English explorer employed by the Dutch East India Company to find a trade route to China, who instead discovered the river that now bears his name

DEWITT CLINTON
1769–1828
American politician who as governor of New York State advocated the construction of the Erie Canal that transformed New York into the busiest port in the United States

30-SECOND TEXT
Andrew Kryzak

3-SECOND SURVEY
New York sits on one of the world's great natural harbours, which has been at the heart of its economic engine for centuries.

3-MINUTE OVERVIEW
The splendours of New York Harbor have not always been limited to its fine aspect and convenience for transportation. Until the early 1900s the harbour and its surrounding waters were home to one of the largest and most fertile systems of oyster beds in the world. New York's working man and the city's elite alike fed on local oysters – and their export made the city famous for bivalves.

One billion gallons of water pass daily through a disinfection facility in Westchester County; the world's largest, it provides New Yorkers with clean drinking water.

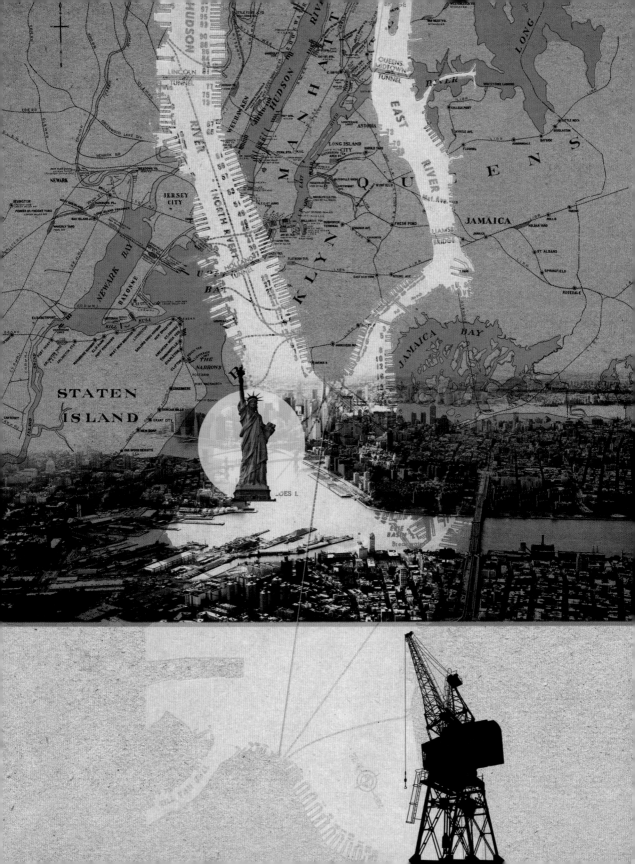

THE GRID

the 30-second tour

In 1811, the New York State legislature adopted what would become the definitive feature of Manhattan's built environment: its street grid. The Commissioners' Plan provided for the entirety of the island to be laid out between 14th Street and Washington Heights in the pattern of avenues and streets that has defined the city ever since. The plan was not only designed for the orderly layout of Manhattan, but also for the efficient speculation on and sale of its property, an early expression of New York's boundless confidence in its own future. Reasoning that 'straight-sided and right-angled houses' were easiest to build and live in, the Commissioners' Plan imposed a straight rectilinear grid on the city's diverse topography, rather than a more varied plan. However, Broadway – which had been the main road through Manhattan since the days of the Dutch, following an older Native American path – was incorporated into the plan, crossing the grid diagonally below 78th Street. And although the original plan made little provision for parkland beyond the few small green squares already extant at the time, the creation of Central Park in the 1850s provided the open space that the Commissioners' Plan had not originally envisaged.

RELATED ENTRIES
See also
PARKS
page 80

URBAN PLANNING
page 82

3-SECOND SURVEY
New York's celebrated grid was laid out in 1811, when the city was still gathered at the tip of Manhattan.

3-MINUTE OVERVIEW
Some pleasures of the grid could not have been anticipated by the commissioners. Twice each year – usually around 28 May and 12 July – the setting sun aligns precisely with the east–west axis of Manhattan's numbered streets. The sun's descent on the horizon is framed by the city's urban canyons, and the curtain walls of the many skyscrapers reflect and refract the light across town. The effect is popularly known as 'the Manhattan solstice' or 'Manhattanhenge'.

3-SECOND BIOGRAPHY
JOHN JACOB ASTOR
1763–1848
German-American businessman who made a fortune in the North American fur trade, then in the 1830s put all his money into New York City land and property development. Late in life, he is reported to have said, 'If I could live all over again, I would buy every square inch of Manhattan.'

30-SECOND TEXT
Andrew Kryzak

Look closely and you'll find neighbourhoods exempt from the grid – notably Greenwich Village, whose 19th-century residents succeeded in preserving their crooked colonial lanes.

RIDING THE RAILS

the 30-second tour

When the New York and Harlem
Railroad opened along the Bowery in 1832,
passengers travelled what was the earliest
streetcar line in the United States. Twenty years
later, that line had been extended 200km
(125 miles) north and was joined by Cornelius
Vanderbilt to his New York Central and Hudson
River Railroad, carrying passengers and freight
into the city. In 1913, the Vanderbilts opened
Grand Central Terminal. Three years earlier, the
competing Pennsylvania Railroad had opened
Pennsylvania Station, whose demolition in 1963
energized the historic preservation movement in
New York. The city's first subway opened in 1904
to relieve overcrowding on Manhattan's surface
transit routes; in the 21st century, the subway
system covers more than 1,050km (650 miles),
linking four of the five boroughs and operating
24 hours per day. Gone, however, are New York's
elevated railroads, developed more than 25
years before the first subway, as are the city's
streetcars, the trolleys that began on the Bowery
in 1832 and inspired the name of the Brooklyn
Dodgers. In addition to the subway, New York's
modern rail passengers are served by Metro-
North Railroad, PATH, New Jersey Transit, the
Staten Island Railway, Amtrak and the Long
Island Rail Road, the oldest American railway
to operate under its original name and charter.

3-SECOND SURVEY
Since the 19th century,
the fastest and easiest
way to travel into
Manhattan and around
town has been by train.

3-MINUTE OVERVIEW
If the famous song 'New
York, New York' from the
1944 musical *On the
Town* is any indication,
the subway makes the
city. New York's rail
transportation network
includes not only the
subway, but also passenger
railroads connecting the
city to its suburbs, upstate
New York and the major
cities of the East Coast.

3-SECOND BIOGRAPHY
CORNELIUS VANDERBILT
1794–1877
American magnate who in
1863 took control of the New
York and Harlem Railroad and
in 1871 built the original
Grand Central Depot as his
railroad's terminus. Upon
his death he left an estate
worth $100 million

30-SECOND TEXT
Andrew Kryzak

*The New York Subway
is the largest rapid
transit system in the
world, opening the
five boroughs up to
all New Yorkers.*

GRIDLOCK ALERT

the 30-second tour

The jaywalking, stiletto-strutting, breakneck pace of life in New York is no myth. And in a town where everyone's in a hurry, it's often easiest to avoid wheels, skip the pricy taxi ride and go by foot. Nevertheless, the iconic yellow cabs (notwithstanding a fleet of apple-green ones serving the outer boroughs and upper Manhattan) make 175 million trips and carry 236 million passengers each year, according to the Taxi and Limousine Commission. And as newer car services proliferate, it has led to a steep climb in traffic – between 2011 and 2015, the number of for-hire vehicles in the city grew by more than 60 per cent. Add in the daily grind of delivery trucks and daily commuters traversing bridges and tunnels to drive into the business districts – short on both parking spaces and loading docks – and it makes for near-chronic gridlock. To help reduce traffic, the city is considering congestion pricing schemes that would add tolls to certain East River bridges that have long been free to drivers, and limit truck deliveries during rush hour. Meanwhile, under mayor Michael Bloomberg, the city worked to reshape its street life in part by repurposing 10.5 hectares (26 acres) of active car lanes into pedestrian zones and introducing the Citi Bike bicycle-sharing programme for commuters who prefer the bell to the horn.

3-SECOND SURVEY
Comedian Johnny Carson once described a 'New York minute' as the moment between a traffic light turning green and the guy behind you honking his horn.

3-MINUTE OVERVIEW
While New York today boasts more car-free households than any other major American city, when the city built its highways in the early and mid 20th century it saw them as a means to progress. Many are part of the legacy of controversial urban planner Robert Moses. In 1934–68 his highway projects (including the Cross Bronx Expressway and Elevated West Side Highway, among others) often disrupted – even destroyed – entire neighbourhoods and increased residents' car dependency.

RELATED ENTRIES
See also
BRIDGES & TUNNELS
page 78

URBAN PLANNING
page 82

3-SECOND BIOGRAPHIES
ROBERT MOSES
1888–1981
City planner whose many initiatives included the region's highway network

JANETTE SADIK-KHAN
1960–
New York transportation commissioner in 2007–13 who reshaped the city's present-day street life with new pedestrian zones, bus-only and bike-only lanes

30-SECOND TEXT
Jennifer Shalant

The last iconic yellow Checker cab was retired in 1999 after more than 20 years of service and nearly a million miles on its odometer.

BRIDGES
& TUNNELS

the 30-second tour

Referring to the 'Bridge and

Tunnel' crowd may be shorthand for separating suburbanites from proper New Yorkers, but the city's famous bridges and tunnels have provided a vital link in knitting the five boroughs into a navigable modern city. The most famous of them all is the Brooklyn Bridge, which opened in 1883 as the 'Great Bridge', one of the marvels of the world. Its construction was instigated following the winter of 1866–67, which saw a frozen East River impede the vital ferry service between the then-independent cities of New York and Brooklyn. The use of steel in a suspension bridge was revolutionary, and provided unprecedented strength and durability. After 20 years alone above the waters, the Brooklyn Bridge was joined by the other East River crossings, each a monument in its own right: the Williamsburg Bridge (1903), the Manhattan Bridge (1909) and the Queensboro Bridge (1909). In 1927, the Holland Tunnel joined the bridges of New York, the first vehicular crossing of the Hudson River and at 2,608m (8,557ft) long an engineering masterpiece. Its ventilation system was a revolution, one that became the model for ventilating other submarine tunnels, including its uptown neighbour, the Lincoln Tunnel, which opened in 1937.

RELATED ENTRY
See also
WATERWAYS
page 70

3-SECOND BIOGRAPHY
EMILY WARREN ROEBLING
1843–1903
Born in Cold Spring, New York, Roebling completed the construction of the Brooklyn Bridge after her husband Washington Roebling, chief engineer on the project, became bedridden

30-SECOND TEXT
Andrew Kryzak

3-SECOND SURVEY
New York, a city of islands, is knitted together and to the mainland by its network of bridges and tunnels.

3-MINUTE OVERVIEW
'I have a bridge to sell you.' It is no coincidence that one of New York's classic lines refers to its most classic bridge. The Brooklyn Bridge is almost unique among New York's spans in providing a pedestrian crossing. Walking across it offers an intimate experience of the bridge and a matchless view of Lower Manhattan and New York Harbor, and indeed the walkway provided a way home for thousands of Brooklynites on 9/11.

According to the Department of Transportation, the Brooklyn Bridge bears the weight of 120,000 vehicle crossings, 4,000 pedestrians and 3,100 cyclists every day.

VITIATED AIR

FRESH AIR

FULL SIZED SECTION
HUDSON RIVER VEHICULAR TUNNEL
DIAMETER 29 FT. 6 IN.

FILLED GROUND

SAND AND GRAVEL

CLAY

SAND AND CLAY

CLAY AND SAND

PARKS

the 30-second tour

RELATED ENTRIES
See also
THE CITY TAKES SHAPE
page 14

THE GRID
page 72

URBAN PLANNING
page 82

New York is a city of more than

1,900 parks, ranging in size and fame from Central Park to pocket parks to large nature reserves sprinkled throughout the five boroughs. Bowling Green, the oldest park in New York, has been providing for the 'delight of the Inhabitants of the City' since first set aside in 1733. Apart from this common green space, however, parks were scarce in New York for the next 125 years. The Commissioners' Plan of 1811 made little provision for parkland in the rigorous gridiron of the Manhattan street grid. As the city expanded northwards, Trinity Church laid out St. John's Park as part of the development of its farm on the West Side, and Samuel Ruggles formed Gramercy Park on the East Side, but both were private pleasure grounds, open only to fee-paying key holders. Together with a few other small parks these spaces formed the only open spaces in a densely settled city. Prospect Park in Brooklyn was opened in 1867. While Central Park's junior, it is by no means its inferior in either beauty or splendour, and in many ways is a more relaxed and peaceful expression than its New York cousin.

3-SECOND SURVEY
Pelham Bay Park in the Bronx – at 1,122 hectares (2,772 acres), the city's largest – contains the site of the Puritan dissident Anne Hutchinson's ill-fated settlement.

3-MINUTE OVERVIEW
In 1857, following a decade of advocacy by leading New Yorkers, construction began on the 315 original hectares (778 acres) of Central Park, transforming scrubland and shantytowns. Running from 59th Street to 110th Street in Manhattan, it remains the most visited city park in the United States – and has fulfilled designer Frederick Law Olmsted's prediction that it would represent a 'democratic development of the highest significance'.

3-SECOND BIOGRAPHIES
FREDERICK LAW OLMSTED
1822–1903
Designer (with Calvert Vaux) of Central Park and Prospect Park

ANNE HUTCHINSON
1591–1643
English-born Puritan who took refuge in New Netherland after being banished from the Massachusetts Bay Colony for her quarrels with the colonial leadership; she and her followers were massacred by local Indians

30-SECOND TEXT
Andrew Kryzak

Central Park's verdant fields, landscaped reservoirs and rocky outcroppings are as emblematic of the city as soaring skyscrapers and crowded subways.

URBAN PLANNING

the 30-second tour

Urban planning emerged in New York as a Progressive Era response to problems with market-driven development, with a focus on thinning out teeming slums and commercial districts. The year 1916 saw the city's first zoning law, limiting the height and bulk of skyscrapers and lofts to allow more light to reach the bottom of 'concrete canyons'. A comprehensive regional plan, prepared by a private civic group and prioritizing new infrastructure, followed in 1929. Planning gained traction after the Second World War thanks to a new federal urban-renewal programme in 1949. Nowhere put the programme to more use than New York. Guided by Robert Moses, the city replaced tenement neighbourhoods with Modernist 'tower in the park' public and middle-income housing complexes, as well as hospitals, colleges and arts venues. Criticized by those displaced and by early gentrifiers such as Jane Jacobs who saw value in old buildings and streetscapes, planning entered a new phase in the 1970s, working with neighbourhoods towards more incremental, inclusive changes. With the return of prosperity and growth, planning today focuses on balancing economic development with neighbourhood preservation, while working to make space for a record-high population that is expected to climb to 9 million by 2040.

3-SECOND SURVEY
New York, with its glittering skyline and onetime slums, may seem to embody unbridled capitalism but urban planning has reshaped the city dramatically.

3-MINUTE OVERVIEW
Urban planning is, at core, an effort to address problems with how the market produces urban space. Initially the target was congestion. When the middle class and industry fled after the Second World War, planning evolved to promote modernization, including freeways and employment in post-industrial sectors such as financial services and the arts. Today planning is focused on new challenges, such as preparing for climate change and the shortage of affordable housing.

RELATED ENTRIES
See also
RIDING THE RAILS
page 74

ARCHITECTURE:
SKYSCRAPERS
page 86

PUBLIC HEALTH
page 94

3-SECOND BIOGRAPHIES
ROBERT MOSES
1888–1981
City planner who served as chairman of the Mayor's Committee on Slum Clearance

JANE JACOBS
1916–2006
Journalist and activist, best known for *The Death and Life of Great American Cities* (1961)

30-SECOND TEXT
Matthew Gordon Lasner

Today's urban planners – Jane Jacobs' heirs – have a particular obligation to help uncover and preserve the small, informal economies embedded within great cities.

14 March 1921
Born in Manhattan,
daughter of physician
Michael Landman,
co-author of the play
A Man of Honor

1941
Graduates BA from
Hunter College

1942
Marries industrial
designer L. Garth
Huxtable

1942–50
Graduate student at New
York University

1946–50
Curatorial assistant for
Architecture & Design,
Museum of Modern Art

1950–51
Fulbright fellow in Italy

1950–63
Contributing editor for
*Progressive Art and
Architecture in America*

1958
Guggenheim fellow

1963–82
Architecture critic for
the *New York Times*

1970
Wins Pulitzer prize for
distinguished criticism

1997–2012
Architecture critic for
the *Wall Street Journal*

7 January 2013
Dies in Manhattan

ADA LOUISE HUXTABLE

It is virtually impossible to

discuss architectural criticism – or even architecture – in New York without considering Ada Louise Huxtable. For 21 years she was the architecture critic of the *New York Times* and a prolific writer on architecture and urban design. Huxtable's incisive pen and sharp wit made her both a popular commentator and a force for applying the highest ideals to the built city.

Ada Louise Landman was born in 1921 in Manhattan. She was raised in a Beaux Arts building, on Central Park West, whose scale and sociability to the street formed part of her ideal of how a building ought to interact with its surroundings. She graduated from Hunter College in 1941 and went on to graduate study at New York University's Institute of Fine Arts. While working at Bloomingdale's selling a furniture line with works by such modernists as Eero Saarinen and Charles Eames, she met L. Garth Huxtable, one of the many young designers who toured the collection, and they married in 1942.

In 1963, after graduate study and years spent as a curatorial assistant for architecture and design at the Museum of Modern Art, Huxtable was invited to become the first full-time architecture critic for the *New York Times*, an offer she initially rejected. Clifton Daniel, the

Times' assistant managing editor, persisted – finally persuading her that there was no one better able to fill the post. In 1970, Huxtable and Marquis W. Childs of the *St. Louis Post-Dispatch* were the inaugural winners of the Pulitzer Prize for Distinguished Criticism or Commentary, she for criticism and he for commentary, and three years later she became only the second woman ever appointed to the editorial board of the *Times*.

Never an ideologue, she was as much a champion of excellence in modern architecture as she was a vociferous detractor of its abominations. She condemned architects and the real-estate industry in equal measure for the construction of ill-considered and what she termed 'antisocial' buildings that reacted clumsily with the cityscape. Though Huxtable was an ardent preservationist, she was always more interested in the sensitive interaction of buildings with their setting – both their built neighbours and the pedestrians on the street – than she was with any single architectural style. No consistent friend of either builders or the promoters of academic architectural orthodoxy, Huxtable was nevertheless beloved of the public, and the popularity of her columns made architectural criticism part of the public dialogue in New York.

Andrew Kryzak

ARCHITECTURE: SKYSCRAPERS

the 30-second tour

Although now common around the world, the skyscraper originated as a local building type in 19th-century New York. As Wall Street bankers like J.P. Morgan forged national corporations, new armies of centrally located office workers were needed to administer them. Aided by the passenger elevator, office buildings, which had first appeared around 1850, quickly reached unprecedented heights, with a race to the top culminating in the Empire State Building in 1931. Although very tall buildings captured the public imagination, they proved impractical: it was too difficult to get workers up and down efficiently. Many, including signature towers such as the Woolworth and Chrysler buildings, derived most of their value as corporate advertisements, not office space. By the 1950s the tall skyscraper was all but a relic. One exception was the World Trade Center, a government project intended to convey confidence in the city in an era of urban crisis – not unlike its post-9/11 replacement, One World Trade Center. Meanwhile, the skyscraper has enjoyed an unexpected resurgence as luxury housing. As New York has become a centre for global real-estate investment, 'supertall' towers such as One57, marketed mainly to rich offshore buyers, have begun reshaping the city's skyline for the first time in 80 years.

RELATED ENTRIES
See also
NYSE & AMEX:
GROWTH & CRASHES
page 54

URBAN PLANNING
page 82

3-SECOND SURVEY
The skyscraper, pioneered in the late 19th century, is New York's chief contribution to global architecture: an achievement befitting the capital of capital.

3-MINUTE OVERVIEW
From Cass Gilbert's neo-Gothic Woolworth Building (1913), whose architectural details had to be exaggerated dramatically to be seen from the street; to William Van Alen's Chrysler Building (1930), with its winged radiator caps and chrome-like crown; to SOM's military-strength One World Trade Center (2014), climbing to a symbolically rich height of 1,776ft (541m), the skyscraper has been synonymous with New York's prowess as a global business centre for more than a century.

3-SECOND BIOGRAPHIES
JOHN PIERPONT MORGAN
1837–1913
Banker and pioneer of the modern corporation

CASS GILBERT
1859–1934
American architect who is best known for the Woolworth Building and the United States Supreme Court Building in Washington, D.C.

WILLIAM VAN ALEN
1883–1954
Brooklyn-born architect, best known for the Chrysler Building

30-SECOND TEXT
Matthew Gordon Lasner

The world's most famous skyscraper, the Empire State Building stands 381m (1,250ft) above Fifth Avenue between 33rd and 34th streets.

ARCHITECTURE: CIVIC & DOMESTIC

the 30-second tour

New York City's density has

challenged domestic architects since at least the 17th century, when Dutch farm- and row houses were constructed on lots 8m (25ft) wide. The British-built, symmetrical red brick of the 18th century lost favour in the 19th to the grandeur of Georgian, Federal and Greek Revival row houses. But New York is really a 20th-century town, the capital city of the American century, which saw the evolution of the city's famous skyline and the transformation of a city of private houses into one of apartment houses. The city monuments in the Beaux Arts tradition, designed by American architects trained in European schools, are numerous – from the façade of the Metropolitan Museum of Art to the grandeur of Grand Central Terminal and the main campus of Columbia University. So, too, are many of the city's great churches, from St. Bartholomew's to the Riverside Church and Cathedral of St. John the Divine, which were all built before the Second World War. The city's most famous skyscrapers were built in a fit of optimism in the same period. Nor did architecture cease after the war: the post-war period gave rise to such modern landmarks as the Seagram Building, Lever House and Lincoln Center, all of which are iconic in their own right.

3-SECOND SURVEY
New York is governed from the oldest city hall in the United States still serving its original purpose: a classical building for a cantankerous city.

3-MINUTE OVERVIEW
In 2014, amidst an unforeseen outcry from book lovers the world over, the New York Public Library scrapped plans to renovate its Fifth Avenue branch. Completed in 1911 by Carrère and Hastings, the building is a Beaux Arts landmark as well a world-class research institution, with a pair of beloved marble lions – Patience and Fortitude – standing guard before it and a majestic reading room that runs roughly the length of two city blocks.

RELATED ENTRIES
See also
RIDING THE RAILS
page 74

ARCHITECTURE:
SKYSCRAPERS
page 86

3-SECOND BIOGRAPHY
STANFORD WHITE
1853–1906
Designer of the Washington Memorial Arch in Washington Square, the second Madison Square Garden and the Metropolitan Club, he was shot dead by the millionaire husband of his lover in 1906 atop the garden that he designed

30-SECOND TEXT
Andrew Kryzak

New York's skyline might be dominated by the skyscraper, but the real heart of the city can be found in the understated architecture of the 19th and early 20th century.

CITY LIFE

21 Club Upmarket restaurant and former speakeasy on West 52nd Street. Established in 1922 in Greenwich Village by cousins Jack Kreindler and Charlie Berns as a way of paying night-school tuition, it settled in its current location in 1929.

Anthora coffee cup Paper coffee cup that is a New York icon. It was designed in 1963 to appeal to Greek coffee-shop owners. It bears an image of a Greek amphora (vase) and the words, in Greek-style capitals: 'We are happy to serve you'.

banh mi Vietnamese street food consisting of a French/Vietnamese baguette with filling.

Big 4 The top four fashion weeks – New York, London, Paris and Milan.

Bloods Largely African-American street gang, founded in 1960s Los Angeles in rivalry with the Crips gang and now found nationwide. Members often wear red and address one another as 'blood'.

bodegas Corner shops found first in Spanish-speaking neighbourhoods; they now serve as grocery stores citywide.

Croton Aqueduct Aqueduct built in 1837–42 that carried water 66km (41 miles) from Croton River in Westchester County into Manhattan, where it was stored in reservoirs.

Flushing Meadow Public park in Queens, site of the 1939 and 1964 World's Fair. Citi Field, home to the New York Mets since 2009, is at the park's north end and the park also contains the United States Tennis Association Billie Jean King National Tennis Center, which hosts the United States Open tennis tournament in August/September each year.

Gay Pride March Officially called the LGBT Pride March, a celebration march held on the last Saturday in June that proceeds down Fifth Avenue to Greenwich Village and passes the Stonewall Inn on Christopher Street, location of the 1969 Stonewall Riots that birthed the modern Gay Rights movement.

Jackson Heights Northwestern part of the borough of Queens that is racially diverse and the home to many people of Latin-American and South Asian heritage. The Queens Pride Parade and festival are held there each June to celebrate LGBTQ pride.

knish Street-food snack of dough with hot filling, typically mashed potato and ground meat with onions, made popular by Jewish immigrants from central Europe.

lox Brined salmon typically served with bagel and cream cheese.

needle exchange programme Public-health programme that provides free syringe needles to intravenous drug users to limit the spread of HIV and hepatitis B.

North and South Brother islands Small islands in the East River between the Bronx and Rikers Island. North Brother Island was the site of a hospital from 1885 until the 1930s. On South Brother Island, brewery magnate Jacob Ruppert (1867–1939), owner of the Yankees from 1915 to his death, had a summer house that burned down in 1909.

Red Hook Neighbourhood in Brooklyn. Its Red Hook Fest with dance and live music is held each June on the Brooklyn waterfront.

Rikers Island Complex of ten jails situated on the island of the same name in the East River between the Bronx and Queens. The island has been used as a jail since descendants of Dutch settler Abraham Rycken, after whom Rikers Island is named, sold it to the city in 1884.

souvlaki and kabobs Typical Greek street food consisting of pieces of skewer-grilled meat and vegetables, often served in pitta bread. Kabobs are known as kebabs in British English.

Tin Pan Alley New York songwriters and music publishers who were the dominant force in popular music in the late nineteenth and early twentieth century. Originally the name referred to their location: West 28th Street between Fifth and Sixth Avenue; it is sometimes said to have come from a derogatory *New York Herald* comment on the sound of the cheap upright pianos on which they were composed was like tin pans banging in an alley.

PUBLIC HEALTH

the 30-second tour

Early public-health efforts

focused on staunching epidemics. City-dwellers infected with Yellow Fever or cholera were evacuated and quarantined on Staten Island. In 1842 the Croton Aqueduct was constructed to provide clean water for drinking and street cleaning. The city removed thousands of pigs (its most effective garbage scavengers) and replaced them with the White Wings – rubbish collectors clothed in white uniforms akin to medical professionals, signifying the connection between hygiene and health. They cleared rubbish, stagnant water, dead animals, and human and animal waste. Jacob Riis' photographs of immigrant ghettos spurred tenement-housing laws resulting in improved ventilation, light, fire escapes and an indoor toilet for every two apartments. New York led the science of bacteriology by the 1900s, with the first municipal laboratory routinely to diagnose disease. In 1947 the city underwent the world's largest rapid vaccination campaign, which saw 6.35 million people injected with the smallpox vaccine in a single month. When Dr Jonas Salk discovered the polio vaccine in 1954, 40,000 New York City schoolchildren participated in the field trial. By the end of the twentieth century, the city had all but eradicated the spread of infectious diseases.

RELATED ENTRIES
See also
ETHNIC VILLAGES ON
THE LOWER EAST SIDE
page 46

URBAN PLANNING
page 82

3-SECOND BIOGRAPHIES
GEORGE E. WARING JR.
1833–98
Sanitation commissioner of New York City from 1895, who implemented the White Wings

MARY MALLON
1869–1938
Better known as 'Typhoid Mary', Irish immigrant and asymptomatic carrier of typhoid fever

30-SECOND TEXT
Cheong Kim

3-SECOND SURVEY
New York's life expectancy rates rose unevenly in the 19th century. Innovative programming has since made the city a leader in public health.

3-MINUTE OVERVIEW
Over the years, public health goals stretched from reaction to prevention and control of infectious disease. More recently it encompassed chronic ailments and targeted urban initiatives including window guards in high rises, food-outlet inspections, rat control and a needle exchange programme. After the 9/11 attack, public health officials tackled the handling and identifying of human remains. Today New York aims to reduce health disparities among its economically and racially diverse population.

Today, the New York City Department of Health maintains some of the strictest rules governing public school immunizations in the United States.

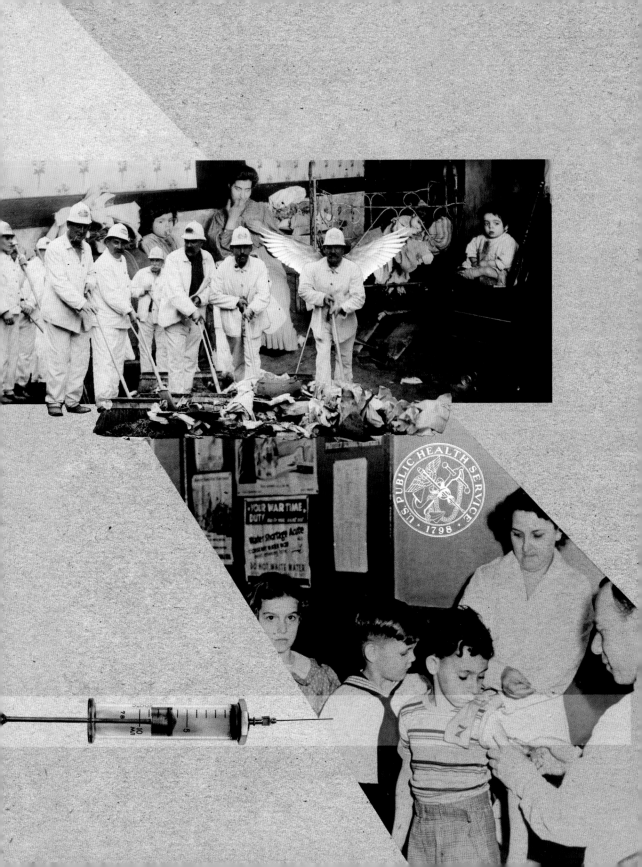

GANGS OF
NEW YORK

the 30-second tour

Anti-Catholic, anti-immigrant

Bowery Boys engaged in more than turf wars with the Irish Dead Rabbits – the groups were political clubs clashing in bloody street battles for votes. Using intimidation and violence, both gangs lobbied for their own candidates, who in turn rewarded constituents with jobs and municipal funds. When the Irish rose out of the slums, they ceded control to the Sicilians. After the Second World War, Italians joined the Five Points Gang to yield a new crop of gangsters. In exchange for *pizzo* – protection money – they safeguarded against the Jewish Eastman Gang and 'smoothed' business transactions, all the while wreaking havoc with widespread robbery, gambling, racketeering and prostitution rings. During Prohibition they turned to bootlegging and, led by the Five Families, stretched their influence to the outer boroughs and beyond. If the Italians had their Mafia, the Chinese had their tongs. Originally conceived as benevolent associations to provide business loans and protect against anti-Chinese harassment, they evolved into secret crime syndicates specializing in gambling, opium distribution and extortion. Today's gangs comprise primarily Hispanic and African-American youth. Still divided along ethnic lines, they remain a primary source of protection from rival gangs.

3-SECOND SURVEY
Both eyes blacked: $3.
Ear chewed off: $15.
Leg or arm broke: $19.
'The big job': $100.
From the Whyos' street-gang menu of services (1860s–90s).

3-MINUTE OVERVIEW
New York street gangs have been driven for centuries by economic, ethnic and political disenfranchisement. Gangs provided a collective political voice, opportunities for financial growth and protection from rival groups. They governed with two hands: one outreached and offering aid, the other a clenched fist under which they ruled. Often working in conjunction with politicians and legitimate businesses, they blurred the lines between empowering and terrorizing their own communities.

RELATED ENTRIES
See also
THE IRISH
page 44

ETHNIC VILLAGES ON THE
LOWER EAST SIDE
page 46

3-SECOND BIOGRAPHIES
HELL-CAT MAGGIE
fl mid-1800s
Early member of the Dead Rabbits, famous for filing her teeth into points and wearing brass fingernails into battle; said to have kept a stash of her victims' ears pickled in alcohol

CHARLES 'LUCKY' LUCIANO
1897–1962
Italian gang leader, the father of modern organized crime, credited with splitting New York City between five families; arrested 25 times

30-SECOND TEXT
Cheong Kim

Disease and gang violence made the tenement houses of nineteenth-century New York City a dangerous place to dwell.

FOOD & DRINK

the 30-second tour

From the colonial coffee houses introduced by the British in 1696 – serving alcohol and political debate alongside coffee – to the Eastern European immigrants hawking pushcart pickles and knishes in the 1860s, the food and drink of New York reflect the immigrant history and multi-ethnic flavour of its population. In the 1970s and 1980s Greeks sold souvlaki and kabobs. The 1990s saw the rise of the ubiquitous bodegas and Korean corner grocers. And though Muslim halal carts may now rule the lunch scene, traffic is riddled with competing trucks selling fusion taco, Belgian waffles or Vietnamese banh mi. What's New York without the delicatessen? Begun on the Lower East Side by late nineteenth-century German and Jewish immigrants, delis now provide flavoured sodas, lox and cured meats citywide. Another Lower East Side star is Chinatown, once a tiny enclave, now trafficked by dumpling-lovers and tourists alike. German-born breweries spawned today's hipster microbreweries of Brooklyn and the Bronx, while mixologists shake and stir small-batch or retro craft-cocktails born of the Prohibition era, which temporarily suppressed the restaurant industry but also gave rise to memorable speakeasies such as the 21 Club.

3-SECOND SURVEY
The bagel, Greek Anthora paper coffee cup, hot dog, pizza slice . . . Is there any other city with as many ethnically diverse, iconic food images?

3-MINUTE OVERVIEW
Immigrants may have brought with them the flavours of their native land, but many dishes originated right here in New York. Delmonico's lays claim to inventing baked Alaska, lobster Newburg and – when it opened in 1827 – the very rituals of American dining. Vichyssoise was first chilled at the Ritz-Carlton, chicken divan the specialty of Divan Parisien, and chicken and waffles married at Well's Restaurant in Harlem. Also New Yorkers are the Manhattan, the Gibson and the Bloody Mary.

RELATED ENTRIES
See also
WELCOME TO NEW YORK
page 42

ETHNIC VILLAGES ON THE
LOWER EAST SIDE
page 46

3-SECOND BIOGRAPHIES
LESLIE BUCK
1922–2010
Designer of the iconic Anthora coffee cup; former paper-cup company executive

DAVID CHANG
1977–
Korean-American chef, writer, founder of popular Momofuku restaurant group

30-SECOND TEXT
Cheong Kim

Embracing its diverse population, New York's delicatessens serve food from the world over, including Jewish, Italian and Greek specialities.

NIGHTLIFE

the 30-second tour

Were he alive today, Peter Stuyvesant – Dutch Director-General of New Netherland until 1664 – would be gratified by the city squares and buildings that bear his name. But having decreed that 'no new taproom, tavern or inn shall be opened', he might be equally scandalized by his city's raucous nightlife. But things were already going downhill by the eighteenth century, when popular evening entertainment centred on private dances for the rich and 'sport' such as bear-baiting and cock-fighting in Ranelagh Gardens. Gambling and folk music filled the numerous nineteenth-century taverns that no decree could keep closed. By 1910, the city's 600 dance halls and 'palaces' rang to black-originated music – Ragtime – performed around the saloons of Tin Pan Alley. Gilded Age robber barons birthed the Met Opera and Broadway, and jazz erupted in Harlem: unlike the more famous Cotton Club, Smalls Paradise accepted black and white patrons alike. In the 1970s and 1980s, glitzy uptown Studio 54, midtown's fashion-focused Xenon and downtown's Mudd Club brought Hollywood to New York City. The East Village's determinedly unglitzy CBGB's gave Patti Smith and Blondie their break in 1974. With the rise of house music, ecstasy and gentrification in the twenty-first century, celebrity DJs now outrank the venue in terms of importance.

3-SECOND SURVEY
Apart from a brief period in the 1970s and 1980s, the city seldom led in creating new music – but nowhere's better to dance to it.

3-MINUTE OVERVIEW
There's something of the seesaw about New York's nightlife. When the city's down, clubs and bars provide a fantastical refuge; when it's thriving, wealth marshals a backlash against perceived noise and nuisance. Elected in 1994, Mayor Rudy Giuliani reenacted a 1926 cabaret law banning dancing in unlicensed premises along with other 'quality of life' initiatives. More recently, Mayor Bloomberg's development of riverside 'light industrial' land has led to the disappearance of many a famous venue.

RELATED ENTRIES
See also
GAY NEW YORK
page 102

COUNTERCULTURAL
NEW YORK
page 108

3-SECOND BIOGRAPHIES
STEVE RUBELL
1943–89
Brooklyn-born mastermind behind the Olympus of New York nightclubs, Studio 54

JUNIOR VASQUEZ
1949–
The DJ's DJ and club acoustic obsessive who founded the influential Sound Factory and Twilo

30-SECOND TEXT
Michael Willoughby

New York nightlife's legendary musicians rarely mind tooting their own horns: George Gershwin attributed his distinctive sound to 'the rising, exhilarating rhythm' of his city.

GAY NEW YORK

the 30-second tour

Borders between 'gay' and
'straight' were porous in the city's early years.
Before marriage, single men mixed more with
other men than with women, their sexuality
denoted more by their own behaviour than
the gender of their partners. In the 1920s,
thousands of spectators travelled to Harlem
for its lavish drag balls. The NYPD intermittently
and brutally enforced laws governing how men
dressed and behaved (including a ban on
'sodomy' until well into the twentieth century)
but a gay world thrived nonetheless via a
network of cafes, rooming-houses and
bathhouses, coded language and looks. Driven
underground during the Depression and then
by McCarthyism, that scene burst into public
consciousness on 28 June 1969, when drag
queens, lesbians, hookers, homeless and
transgender youths – fed up with being shaken
down for cash by the Mafia and corrupt police
– rioted at Greenwich Village tavern, the
Stonewall Inn. A coke-fuelled gay scene led the
city's nightlife in the 1970s: picture Andy Warhol
holding court at Max's Kansas City club before
heading unruffled uptown for the disco at
Studio 54. The first cases of AIDS reported in
the city, in 1981, changed that scene forever.

RELATED ENTRIES
See also
NYPD BLUES
page 58

NIGHTLIFE
page 100

3-SECOND BIOGRAPHIES
JAMES BALDWIN
1924–87
Harlem-born African-
American essayist and
author of pioneering gay
novel, *Giovanni's Room*

SYLVIA RAE RIVERA
1951–2002
Hispanic-American drag queen,
present at the Stonewall Riots
and founding member of both
the Gay Liberation Front and
the Gay Activists Alliance

30-SECOND TEXT
Michael Willoughby

In June 1970, the **New
York Times** *reported on
the city's first Gay-
Pride Parade, in which
thousands marched
from Sheridan Square
to Sheep Meadow.*

3-SECOND SURVEY
Long a hub of the gay
world, New York played
host to a now-vanished
cultural tapestry of
language, dress and
venue for centuries
before Stonewall.

3-MINUTE OVERVIEW
By 1994, New York City had
witnessed 50,000 deaths
from AIDS (new drugs
helped those numbers
plunge the next year).
Shared pain – not least at
their government's inertia
– helped create community
and convince a hostile
nation of that community's
essential humanity. Having
endured punishment of
biblical ferocity, the city's
estimated 765,000 LGBT
people now see their
marriage notices in the
New York Times. Their
rights acknowledged, lives
largely assimilated, their
city may be more humdrum
without the high drama.

GAY RIGHTS

REGISTER & VOTE

Bill Board Courtesy of MAN's Country - NYPAC-N.Y. N.Y.

5 May 1864
Born Elizabeth Jane Cochran in Cochran's Mills, Pennsylvania

1879
Enrols at Indiana State Normal School, Indiana, PA, to study teaching; leaves after one term due to insufficient funds

1885
Hired by the *Pittsburg Dispatch* after submitting an enraged letter to the editor; given pen-name 'Nellie Bly'

1885
Leaves for Mexico on a six-month stint as a foreign correspondent

1887
'10 Days in the Madhouse' appears in the *New York World*, uncovering mistreatment at Blackwell Island

1889–1890
Travels 34,990km (21,740 miles) in 72 days, six hours, 11 minutes breaking the record of Phileas Fogg, the character of Jules Verne's novel *Around the World in Eighty Days*

1894
Reports on the Pullman Strike for *New York World*

1895
Marries Robert Seaman after two-week courtship

1901
Files United States patent 697,553 for a novel milk can

1902
Files United States patent 703,711 for a stacking garbage can

1904
Becomes owner of Iron Clad Manufacturing after the death of her husband Robert Seaman

1914
Files for bankruptcy and flees to Austria to avoid debtors; covers the First World War as the United States' first female war correspondent

1919
Returns to the United States to write advice columns for the *Evening Journal* and advocates for orphaned children and the poor

27 January 1922
Dies of pneumonia at the age of 57; journalist Arthur Brisbane describes her in the *Evening Journal* as the best reporter in America

NELLIE BLY

Nellie Bly – pioneer of stunt

journalism and investigative reporting – lived a life as sensational as her articles. Born Elizabeth Cochran on 5 May 1864, she was the 13th child of the county judge in Cochran's Mills, Pennsylvania. Her father's death plummeted the family into poverty, forcing a move to Pittsburgh where her mother would run a boarding house. Her journalism career began when, enraged by a column in the *Pittsburg Dispatch* calling working women 'a monstrosity', Elizabeth's fiery rebuttal elicited a job offer and the pen name 'Nellie Bly', (misspelled) after the Stephen Foster song.

While other female journalists covered fashion and gardening, Bly capitalized on the reformist trend and women's suffrage movement. Employing intricate detail and personal opinion, she reported on working-class women and the poor – joining an assembly line to write on sweatshops, masquerading as an unwed mother to uncover baby-buying schemes, travelling to Mexico as a foreign correspondent to cover protests against Porfirio Díaz.

In 1887, Bly went undercover for Joseph Pulizter's *New York World*, feigning insanity to glimpse the brutality and neglect at the Women's Lunatic Asylum on Blackwell's Island. Her report triggered a grand jury investigation and an $850,000 increase in corrections spending. But Bly's most celebrated 'stunt' was travelling around the globe to break the record of Phileas Fogg, the fictional character of Jules Verne's *Around the World in Eighty Days*. She met Verne in Amiens, visited a leper colony in China and acquired a pet monkey in Singapore. A contest to predict her return date drew more than half a million entries; she spawned trading cards and a board game. On 25 January 1890, Bly returned to celebratory gunshots ending her journey after 72 days, six hours and 11 minutes.

At the age of 31, Bly married millionaire industrialist Robert Seaman, 40 years her senior. Upon his death Bly took over his Ironclad Manufacturing Co. She held two United States patents and was a leading female industrialist before employee embezzlement forced the company into bankruptcy. Averting financial woes, Bly fled to Austria at the onset of the First World War, and ended up reporting from the trenches as the United States' first female war correspondent.

In 1919, she returned to New York as a columnist for the *Evening Journal* and worked tirelessly with orphans, adopting a child at age 57. In 1922 Bly died of pneumonia and is interred in Woodlawn Cemetery in the Bronx.

Cheong Kim

BAGPIPES
& BALLOONS
the 30-second tour

On any summer weekend, you can stroll the Upper West Side or Lower East Side and find traffic-free plazas lined with booths offering treats and trinkets for sale. Street fairs are a deeply rooted New York tradition – even the colonists of New Amsterdam traded outside the Dutch West India Company's storehouses. Today, these street events serve more as gathering spots than places to purchase staples. But New York's fairs don't just serve the locals. In 1939 and 1965, more than 90 million spectators came to Flushing Meadows, Queens, to view the expos of the World's Fair, presenting brighter visions of tomorrow in the face of unfolding world war and various national crises. If not quite as massive, many of New York's annual parades draw impressive crowds – 2 million spectators line the streets for the St. Patrick's Day march up Fifth Avenue, a tradition dating from 1762, and 3.5 million take in the giant balloons of the Macy's Thanksgiving Day Parade, marking the official start of the city's holiday season since 1924. At the opposite end of the spectrum, lowbrow street-side spectacles, from the 'Naked Cowboy' of current-day Times Square to P.T. Barnum, the mid nineteenth-century showman who put human oddities and exotic animals on display, have left their marks on the city's performance culture.

RELATED ENTRIES
See also
GAY NEW YORK
page 102

COUNTERCULTURAL
NEW YORK
page 108

3-SECOND BIOGRAPHIES
P.T. BARNUM
1810–91
American showman, promoter of hoaxes and sideshow curiosities

CRAIG RODWELL
1940–83
Gay-rights activist and resident of Manhattan's Greenwich Village, a leader of the Stonewall Rebellion, and one of the promoters of the first Gay Pride March in New York

30-SECOND TEXT
Jennifer Shalant

Ticker-tape parades – during which shredded paper is showered onto a parade route from surrounding buildings – originated with the October 1886 dedication to Lady Liberty.

3-SECOND SURVEY
Another Sunday (or Monday, Tuesday or Wednesday . . .), another parade or fair marks the calendar of the city that never sleeps.

3-MINUTE OVERVIEW
Many of New York's parades – including the National Puerto Rican Day Parade, Pride March and Lunar New Year Festival – celebrate the diverse cultures that define this city. Some have even arisen in response to one another, like Queens' St. Pat's for All Parade, which began after gay and lesbian groups were banned from marching in the Manhattan event. For spectators and passers-by alike, there are fewmore direct ways to get to know your neighbours.

COUNTERCULTURAL NEW YORK

the 30-second text

New York City was the first political capital of the United States, but it was not destined to remain so, becoming the cultural – and consequently countercultural – capital instead. By the time Theodore Roszak coined the term in 1969, the city had long been a magnet to those it described. American bohemianism got its start in pre-Civil War New York. Flappers danced defiantly in Jazz Age speakeasies and Beat Generation writers Allen Ginsberg and Jack Kerouac met uptown. New York School painters Mark Rothko and Jackson Pollock introduced the post-war art world to an audaciously abstract expressionism. Roszak intended the term specifically to capture the values of anti-Vietnam War activists and members of the New Left who rejected the social conventions of their parents' generation and gathered in Greenwich Village. If the city's distinguished theatres and museums are emblems of its cultural standing, equal evidence abounds of sustained resistance to those standards, from cheerfully pierced patrons flipping through the stacks at St. Mark's Place Comics to monks break-dancing in Union Square, improvisational theatre off-Broadway and musicians performing in the bowels of the subway – all are testimony to the continued vitality of the city's counterculture.

RELATED ENTRIES
See also
ART: ARTISTS, CRITICS, GALLERIES, STREET ART
page 120

CLASSICAL CITY
page 138

3-SECOND BIOGRAPHIES
EMMA GOLDMAN
1869–1940
Russian-born anarchist who made her name in Manhattan with fiery oration on behalf of workers and women

W.H. AUDEN
1907–73
Anglo-American poet, briefly shared Brooklyn Heights writers' haven with Carson McCullers and Benjamin Britten before living at 77 St. Mark's Place for nearly 20 years

30-SECOND TEXT
Sarah Fenton

3-SECOND SURVEY
Bemoaning the death of their city's counterculture is the job of ageing New Yorkers; remaking that culture with brazen impertinence, the task of its youth.

3-MINUTE OVERVIEW
When it opened in 1884, the 12-storey Chelsea Hotel was the tallest building in the city. It still remains the byword of its counterculture – the site of Dylan Thomas's last days and Robert Mapplethorpe's first photographs; where William Burroughs wrote *Naked Lunch* and Andy Warhol filmed *Chelsea Girls*. Leonard Cohen and Bob Dylan immortalized it in song while Nancy Spungen (girlfriend of Sex Pistol Sid Vicious) died there – signaling, some believe, the death of Punk itself.

Playwright Arthur Miller called the Chelsea Hotel 'the high spot of the surreal . . . no vacuum cleaners, no rules and no shame.'

FASHIONABLE NEW YORK

the 30-second tour

Prior to the start of the

nineteenth century, households in the United States were responsible for creating their own clothes; only the conspicuously wealthy sought out tailors. This changed with slavery, when large quantities of inexpensive, durable clothing were required to dress entire labour forces. With Elias Howe's refinement of the sewing machine in the mid 1800s, and the arrival of skilled immigrants, New York's manufacturing industry was born. The Garment District was the epicentre – 2.5 square km (1 sq mile), stretching from 35th to 41st streets, between Fifth and Ninth avenues. Here the fraternity of tailors gave way to factories filled with German and Irish seamstresses who not only mass-produced uniforms for prospectors, sailors and Civil War troops but learned to recreate French fashions for an American audience. By 1910, 70 per cent of clothing worn by American women originated in the Garment District, but it was not until the Second World War, when Americans could no longer access Paris' catwalks, that it became the hotbed of American fashion. With publicist Eleanor Lambert and *Vogue* editors Diana Vreeland and Anna Wintour, American fashion grew not just to reflect Parisian styles, but to shape the glamorous trends of today. New York's Fashion Week is now one of the 'Big 4.'

3-SECOND SURVEY
An industry born of necessity, New York's fashion scene now rules the catwalk and sets the pattern for international trends.

3-MINUTE OVERVIEW
The first department stores sold all manner of dry goods and were clustered along lower Manhattan's 'Ladies Mile'. With the advent of manufacturing and American fashions, stores began to migrate north to Fifth Avenue, once regarded as the world's most expensive and luxurious shopping street. While many of the department stores have since merged or closed, glittering examples of high style and luxury still prevail at Bergdorf Goodman, Saks Fifth Avenue and Henri Bendel.

RELATED ENTRIES
See also
WELCOME TO NEW YORK
page 42

NEWSPAPERS & MAGAZINES
page 126

3-SECOND BIOGRAPHIES
ELEANOR LAMBERT
1903–2003
Influential American art and fashion publicist, creator of New York Fashion Week, the International Best Dressed List, cofounder of MOMA

ANNA WINTOUR
1949–
British-born fashion icon, editor-in-chief of American *Vogue* since 1988

30-SECOND TEXT
Cheong Kim

Can't afford the ticket to Fashion Week? No problem: visit Soho or 7th Avenue to witness the city's signature mix of glamour and grit.

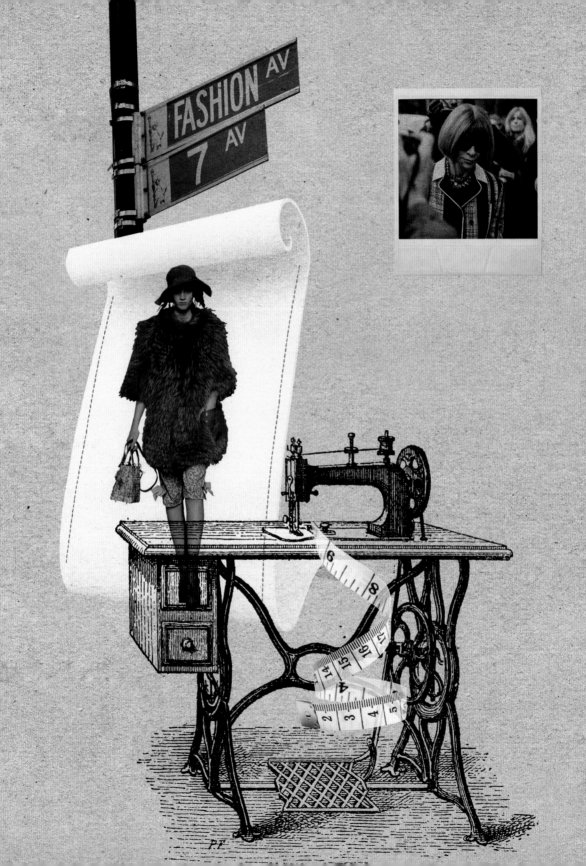

EDUCATING THE CITY

the 30-second tour

The massive undertaking of educating New York City's youth falls primarily to the City's public school system, the largest in the United States. The public system serves almost 1 million students in 1,800 schools, and has an annual operating budget of nearly $22 billion. It is led by the schools chancellor, who is appointed by the mayor, in cooperation with a citywide panel of advisers and borough-level education councils. Schools receive funding from a variety of federal, state and local sources. During the 2013–14 school year, nearly 79 per cent of public schools received Title 1 funds for serving low-income student populations. The New York City public schools provide a dizzying array of programmes and services to support all kinds of students, including English-language learners, students with disabilities, homeless children and students who may have dropped out of school. The city is divided up into 32 geographic districts that are then split into smaller zones that determine school assignment. Although students are assigned to local schools based on their residential address, an extensive school choice policy allows residents to apply to schools outside of their district. Additionally, nearly 900 secular and private schools operate independently of the public system.

3-SECOND SURVEY
The first public school in Manhattan, P.S. 1, opened in 1806. Replicated across the five boroughs, the number-naming system produced considerable confusion and five P.S. 1s.

3-MINUTE OVERVIEW
New York City is also home to more university students than any other city in the United States. Its 110 institutions of higher education include the expansive public City University of New York (CUNY) system; private universities such as Columbia (the state's oldest, founded by royal charter in 1754) and New York University; private religious institutions such as Fordham, St. John's and Yeshiva universities; and the Juilliard School.

RELATED ENTRIES
See also
URBAN PLANNING
page 82

PUBLIC HEALTH
page 94

3-SECOND BIOGRAPHIES
JAMES MCCUNE SMITH
1813–65
The first African American to hold a degree in medicine; he attended the African Free School in Manhattan

CHARLES B.J. SNYDER
1860–1945
American architect and superintendent of school buildings who designed or renovated more than 350 schools, at least 13 of them now designated landmarks

30-SECOND TEXT
Nancy Green Saraisky

The American Revolution forced an eight-year suspension at King's College. After the war, the University was triumphantly reopened with a new name: Columbia.

ART & CULTURE

ART & CULTURE
GLOSSARY

abolitionism Movement to end slavery.

Bushwick Neighbourhood in Brooklyn bordering Williamsburg, Brownsville and Bedford-Stuyvesant with a very strong and active community of artists.

Chelsea West Side neighbourhood traditionally known for its active gay scene and since the 1990s as a hub for contemporary art. It is home to the iconic Chelsea Hotel, where poet Dylan Thomas fell seriously ill and Nancy Spungen, girlfriend of Sex Pistol Sid Vicious, died, and writers and musicians including Brendan Behan, Bob Dylan, Leonard Cohen and Patti Smith lived. The area was named after the manor of Chelsea in London by its eighteenth-century owner Thomas Clarke, a retired major.

The Great White Way Section of Broadway in Midtown between 42nd Street and 53rd Street, home to the 'Theater District' and including Times Square. The phrase was originally applied to a slightly different section of Broadway because it was so brightly lit by electrical advertising at the close of the nineteenth century.

Greenwich Village Area in the West Side of Lower Manhattan, for many decades New York's principal centre for visual artists, writers and bohemian life. The 50s Beat movement, 60s counterculture and modern LGBT movement had their birth in the area locals call simply 'the Village', which is bounded by 14th Street, Houston Street, Broadway and the East River. The name comes from Dutch Groenwijck, meaning 'Green District'.

The High Line Elevated 'greenway' park on an abandoned West Side railway spur, opened in phases between 2009 and September 2014. It runs 2.33km (1.45 miles) from Gansevoort Street in the Meatpacking District to West 34th Street.

Jazz Age Period in the 1920s when jazz music and dance became popular in the United States and Europe. Sometimes known as 'the Roaring Twenties', the period came to a shuddering halt with the Wall Street Crash of 1929 and the economic gloom of the Great Depression (1929–39).

Meatpacking District Once the home of New York's meat-handling warehouses and markets, this area is now an ultra-glamorous, 24-hour venue, with nightclubs, restaurants, chic boutiques and vastly expensive housing – as well as a section of the High Line park and recently opened Whitney Museum of American Art. It is bounded by West 14th Street and Gansevoort Street between Hudson Street and the Hudson River, and is officially known as Gansevoort Market.

Morningside Heights Area on the Upper West Side sometimes described as 'Greater Harlem', home to Columbia University and the Cathedral of St. John the Divine. Beat writers Jack Kerouac and Allen Ginsberg lived there, as did F. Scott Fitzgerald for a while – and George Gershwin wrote *Rhapsody in Blue* in the area. Local diner Tom's Restaurant inspired the Suzanne Vega song 'Tom's Diner' and featured in the exterior shots for the café frequented by Jerry, George, Elaine and Kramer in TV comedy *Seinfeld*.

SoHo Neighbourhood in Lower Manhattan, nicknamed for its location 'South of Houston Street.' It is best known for its cast-iron architecture and as the first New York neighborhood that experienced artist-led gentrification. In the 1960s the area was to be the site of the Lower Manhattan Expressway planned by Robert Moses, but the author and civic activist Jane Jacobs and local residents challenged the scheme. From the 1960s SoHo was home to artists who used abandoned manufacturing and commercial buildings as live/work spaces – the pioneers of loft living. Today it is known above all for shopping.

Williamsburg Neighbourhood in Brooklyn bordering Bedford-Stuyvesant, much gentrified since the 1990s, when many artists moved to the area, and in the early twenty-first century a hub for indie rock and hipster culture – nicknamed 'Little Berlin'.

ART: MUSEUMS

the 30-second tour

In 1930 Gertrude Vanderbilt

Whitney offered the Metropolitan Museum of Art (Met) her private collection of 700 paintings and the funds for a wing to house them. Rejecting the tenets of modern art, the Met declined her offer, inspiring Whitney to open her eponymous museum. Today, the Whitney Museum of American Art showcases the work of every important living American artist of the twentieth century, and its Whitney Biennial sets the tone for contemporary art – influencing trends and heralding works by new American artists. Its establishment was not the only time modern art was snubbed in NY: Abby Aldrich Rockefeller might have been the wife of John D. Rockefeller, Jr., but he was so opposed to modern art that he refused to help finance the launch of the Museum of Modern Art (MoMA). Among the first to include all manner of visual expression, MoMA now houses 200,000 works from international artists spanning the last 150 years. Rockefeller eventually came around to become one of the MoMA's greatest benefactors. In 1987, even the majestic Met – the largest art museum in the United States; home to ancient Greek and Roman antiquities, 2,500 European paintings and the most Egyptian art outside of Cairo – inaugurated the Lila Acheson Wallace Wing of modern art.

RELATED ENTRY
See also
ART: ARTISTS, CRITICS, GALLERIES, STREET ART
page 120

3-SECOND SURVEY
Whether your tastes veer towards antiquities or postmodernism, New York's museums boast some of the finest and most extensive collections of art in existence.

3-MINUTE OVERVIEW
The Guggenheim Museum debuted in 1939 in a former automobile showroom as the Museum of Non-Objective Painting. Today its impressive collection of abstract art is housed in Frank Lloyd Wright's modernist concrete spiral on Fifth Avenue. Upon his death, industrialist Henry Clay Frick opened the doors of his mansion, a jewel-box of expertly curated European treasures to become The Frick, one of America's preeminent small museums. These two iconic settings are as magnificent as the works within them.

3-SECOND BIOGRAPHIES
ABBY ALDRICH ROCKEFELLER
1874–1948
American socialite and philanthropist, wife of John D. Rockefeller, Jr., and driving force behind the creation of MoMA

GERTRUDE VANDERBILT WHITNEY
1875–1942
American sculptor, collector, art patron and founder of the Whitney Museum of American Art

30-SECOND TEXT
Cheong Kim

Museums balance the responsibility to expose more people to more art with the need to maintain a sacred space in which to contemplate it.

ART: ARTISTS, CRITICS, GALLERIES, STREET ART

the 30-second tour

No city crams more art into a smaller area than New York. This density allowed it to grow from a leading nineteenth-century arts centre to the capital of the art world after 1945. New York's art community has long been centred in Lower Manhattan. The Tenth Street Studio Building was home to Winslow Homer and helped launch Greenwich Village as the city's leading art district. Gertrude Vanderbilt Whitney's Greenwich Village studio evolved into the Whitney Museum of American Art. In the 1940s and '50s, the New York School of Abstract Expressionism coalesced on Eighth Street in the Village. With the help of critic Clement Greenberg and patron Peggy Guggenheim, Jackson Pollock, Willem de Kooning, and Mark Rothko launched their careers over drinks at the Cedar Tavern. In the 1970s, artists and galleries moved to the lofts of SoHo. These cavernous spaces housed interdisciplinary performance artists such as Gordon Matta-Clark and Trisha Brown. In the 1980s, Keith Haring and Jean-Michel Basquiat moved from the East Village streets to galleries and museums, bringing street art into the formal art world. After moving uptown from 1954 to 2015, the Whitney Museum is back downtown in the Meatpacking District, a few blocks from the city's most concentrated gallery district in west Chelsea.

3-SECOND BIOGRAPHIES
ANDY WARHOL
1928–87
American artist who pioneered
Pop Art from his Factory

JEAN-MICHEL BASQUIAT
1960–88
American artist, initially a
graffiti artist who tagged
'Samo' on New York buildings;
later his works became part
of the permanent collection
at MoMA

30-SECOND TEXT
Aaron Shkuda

English writer Peter Shaffer has said that 'If London is a watercolour, New York is an oil painting.'

BROADWAY

the 30-second tour

When the British took control of New York in 1664, they brought with them a rich tradition of theatre. The original shows were Shakespearian plays and operas staged in lower Manhattan, often performed by troupes imported from London. After a brief hiatus during the Revolutionary War, theatre returned, eschewing Britain and its serious theatrical performances for lighter fare: P. T. Barnum's circus, magicians, burlesque, the uniquely American blackface minstrel, extravagant operas and vaudeville – varied acts loosely bound by song and dance, and presented under the same bill. In 1899, Oscar Hammerstein ventured north and built the 1,000-seat Victoria Theater on West 42nd St. Other theatres soon followed and The Great White Way was born. In the Roaring Twenties, Florenz Ziegfeld revamped the variety show to create the glittering, spectacular song-and-dance revues that would set the scope for future productions. Over the years Broadway has survived numerous wars, the rise of motion pictures and the Great Depression to endure as one of the city's most lucrative tourist attractions. And while today's Broadway boasts 40 theatres showcasing all genres, theatregoers' preferences remain unchanged: 23 of the top 25 longest running Broadway shows are musicals.

3-SECOND SURVEY
From its origins in opera and vaudeville, New York's blockbuster musical still shines on Broadway.

3-MINUTE OVERVIEW
When the Commissioners' Plan of 1811 reconfigured New York into its now famous grid system, one of the few roads spared was Broadway, an old Indian Wickquasgeck Trail that snaked down nearly the entire course of the island. It is from this diagonal strip, between 41st and 53rd streets, and Sixth and Ninth avenues, that one of the world's most celebrated theatre districts reigns.

RELATED ENTRIES
See also
THE GRID
page 72

RIDING THE RAILS
page 74

3-SECOND BIOGRAPHIES
OSCAR HAMMERSTEIN
1895–1960
New York-born theatrical producer, musical director, winner of two Pulitzer Prizes, five Tony Awards and two Academy Awards for Best Original Song

STEPHEN SONDHEIM
1930–
Celebrated New York-born composer and lyricist, recipient of eight Grammy Awards, the Pulitzer Prize, an Academy Award and the most Tony Awards (eight) of any composer

30-SECOND TEXT
Cheong Kim

On the Town, West Side Story, Hair, A Chorus Line, Annie, Rent, Hamilton: *musicals are not just shown in New York but set here too.*

HARLEM RENAISSANCE

the 30-second tour

The Harlem Renaissance was

a literary, social and artistic movement that peaked during the late 1920s in the predominantly black milieu of Harlem in Manhattan. In the first decades of the twentieth century, as Harlem became a destination for those migrating out of the South, the neighbourhood was established as the home of New York's black middle class and cultural élite. The literati vigorously debated politics, folk culture, sexual freedom and literary tradition, while the growing popularity of black culture in 1920s New York brought these issues before a wider public. The major exponent of the Harlem Renaissance was the ideal of the so-called 'New Negro', who through espousing pride in his race and the literary, social and artistic products of the explicitly African-American movement, could and would challenge the racism prevalent within American society. Leading lights of the Harlem Renaissance included writers W.E.B. Du Bois, Zora Neale Hurston, poet Langston Hughes, political leader Marcus Garvey and lawyer and diplomat James Weldon Johnson. Organizations to promote black political interests such as the National Urban League and the the National Association for the Advancement of Colored People (NAACP) were established and flourished during the period.

3-SECOND SURVEY
It was not until the 1921 production of *Shuffle Along* that an all-black musical finally was produced on the Broadway stage.

3-MINUTE OVERVIEW
Although the Harlem Renaissance overlapped with the Jazz Age in New York, iconic black performers such as Duke Ellington, Louis Armstrong and Bessie Smith are not commonly considered to have been part of the movement. As whites came uptown to venues such as the Cotton Club, however, 'black' music helped propel African-American culture into the popular imagination.

RELATED ENTRIES
See also
AFRICAN AMERICANS IN NEW YORK
page 40

LITERARY CITY:
NEW YORK STORIES
page 130

3-SECOND BIOGRAPHIES
JAMES WELDON JOHNSON
1871–1938
Florida-born black American author and lawyer who settled in New York and became a leading light of the Harlem Renaissance and the NAACP

LANGSTON HUGHES
1902–67
Black American 'jazz poet', novelist and leader of the Harlem Renaissance

30-SECOND TEXT
Andrew Kryzak

Musicians and novelists, painters, political theorists and poets — the artists and artifacts of the Harlem Renaissance were so varied and ambitious as to defy categorization.

NEWSPAPERS & MAGAZINES

the 30-second tour

RELATED ENTRIES
See also
THE ENGLISH
page 36

LITERARY CITY: NEW YORK
STORIES
page 130

3-SECOND SURVEY
What's a morning
commute without a bagel,
a cup of coffee and a
folded-over copy of the
New York Times?

3-MINUTE OVERVIEW
In December 1962, 17,000
employees stopped the
presses for the New York
papers, demanding
increased wages and a halt
to the introduction of
computerized typesetting.
The strike lasted for 114
days and left 600 million
newspapers unprinted;
models stood in storefront
windows holding
chalkboards displaying
daily discounts. Weddings
and funerals went
unannounced. Journalists
turned to other literary
endeavours and advertisers
shifted to television. The
short segment newscast
was extended to a half
hour. The first all-news
radio station was born.

Neither impartial nor current,
the *New York Gazette* became its city's first
newspaper in November 1725: two crudely printed
pages packed with foreign news. Critical of the
Gazette's royalist sympathies, the *New York
Weekly Journal* launched, earning German-born
publisher John Peter Zenger a libel trial and a jail
sentence. By the 1830s a penny press blanketed
the city in tabloid-style newspapers priced well
below the traditional six cents. The cheaper price
garnered a new readership: immigrants, and the
working and middle classes. Publishers kept
articles concise, used straightforward vocabulary
and emphasized crime reports, gossip and other
human-interest stories. The favourable price and
public obsession with crime and crisis spawned
the dailies, forever shaping the speed and
efficiency of American journalism. By the 1920s
news-hungry New Yorkers supported no less
than 19 dailies. Today objectivity reigns at the
nationally esteemed *New York Times* and *Wall
Street Journal*, but no less popular are the
tabloids – the *Daily News*, *Daily Mirror* and *New
York Post*. For higher-brow fare, there's *The
New York Review of Books* long-form essays
from established writers; *New York Magazine*
for culture and lifestyle; and *The New Yorker*,
long regarded as the nation's premier publisher
of short fiction and poetry.

3-SECOND BIOGRAPHIES
HORACE GREELEY
1811–72
Politically active newspaper
editor; his abolitionist
Herald printed 135,000 copies
a day by 1861, and statues of
him still adorn Herald Square
and City Hall

BERTRAM POWERS
1922–2006
Union leader and driving force
behind the newspaper strike
of 1962–63

30-SECOND TEXT
Cheong Kim

*The history of print
journalism is at a
crossroads once again,
as the digital landscape
has transformed
the way that city-
dwellers purchase
and consume news.*

31 May 1819
Born in West Hills, New York; the second son of Walter and Louisa Van Velsor Whitman

1823
Whitman family moves to Brooklyn

1841
Leaves teaching to pursue journalism

1846
Becomes editor of the widely read newspaper the *Brooklyn Daily Eagle*

1855
Self-publishes 795 copies of *Leaves of Grass*, a collection of 12 poems

1862
Travels to Fredericksburg in search of his brother, a Union soldier

1865
Publishes *Drum-Taps* and its sequel, poetic accounts of the war that include the elegy for President Lincoln, 'When Lilacs Last in the Dooryard Bloom'd'

1871
Publishes new collection, *Democratic Vistas*

1873
Suffers a stroke and moves to his brother's home in Camden, New Jersey

26 March 1892
Dies in Camden, aged 72; more than 1,000 people will attend the funeral of 'the good grey poet'

WALT WHITMAN

New York in the nineteenth century smelled of melting lead, overflowing outhouses, long-dead animals – and live ones, too. Hardly the stuff of poetry, but that's precisely what Walt Whitman made of it. A man who believed his own 'arm pits' had an 'aroma finer than prayer' would pay no heed to literary conventions. Unconstrained by rules of rhyme or metre, Whitman invented a new poetic form and opened it to a range of topics long deemed unsuitable for poetry – free verse for a free people. In 1844 the nation's foremost scholar, Ralph Waldo Emerson, argued that 'the experience of each new age requires a new confession, and the world seems always waiting for its poet.' New York was that world; Whitman that poet.

One of eight surviving children in a family of farmers, Whitman was born on Long Island but raised mostly and restlessly in Brooklyn. Pulled out of school at 11 to help support his family, Whitman had little formal education but many jobs – from teaching to newspaper reporting and printing, building and nursing. His strong political feelings (including his commitments to the rights of women, immigrants and the abolition of slavery) and even stronger language made keeping jobs difficult. The effects of intermittent unemployment discouraged Whitman, but were a boon to his legacy: out of a dry spell in the late 1840s came *Leaves of Grass*, which remains the most influential book of poetry written by an American. First published in 1855, the book was revised and added to for the rest of Whitman's life. What began as a book of 12 poems grew to more than 400, including 'Mannahatta', which celebrates 'the place encircled by many swift tides and sparkling waters. How fit a name for America's great democratic island city ... glistening in sunshine, with such New World atmosphere, vista and action!' Whitman mailed Emerson a first edition of the book, to which Emerson responded: 'I greet you at the beginning of a great career.'

And great that career was – 'I am large,' Whitman wrote, 'I contain multitudes.' It included nursing Civil War veterans with unsqueamish devotion – the closest he came to realizing that 'universal brotherhood' he believed was the promise of America. The frankness and carnality with which Whitman would 'sing the body electric' in worshipful odes to the bodies of boys, men and women made his poetry scandalous in his own time but remarkably germane to ours.

Sarah Fenton

LITERARY CITY: NEW YORK STORIES

the 30-second tour

3-SECOND SURVEY

New York's stories don't simply reflect the city; they inform our experience of it. We share the streets, subway and storefronts with the characters of our favourite novels.

3-MINUTE OVERVIEW

Brooklyn-born Maurice Sendak believed that 'fantasy' was a child's tool 'for taming Wild Things'. Well acquainted with all things wild, New York's children are well served by audacious literature: from the gleefully harrowing life of *Stuart Little* (1945) to the anxieties of immigrant parents in *The Cricket in Times Square* (1960). Pint-sized *Eloise* (1955) rules the Plaza; adolescent *Harriet the Spy* (1964) stares down loneliness. For innocence, follow sweet Peter through *The Snowy Day* (1962).

A tour of New York's novels might begin in the Westchester of Washington Irving's youth, which shaped not only his ghostly short story 'The Legend of Sleepy Hollow' (1820) but also the satirical *A History of New York* (1809). Find his successors in satire further south and centuries later: Tom Wolfe – whose *The Bonfire of the Vanities* (1987) gives a star turn to a Bronx highway – and Don DeLillo, whose *Underworld* (1997) sails south into Washington Heights, where James Baldwin's Rufus plunged off the George Washington Bridge into *Another Country* (1962). On Manhattan's Upper East Side, beautiful girls sell their souls for treasure in Edith Wharton's *The House of Mirth* (1905) and Truman Capote's *Breakfast at Tiffany's* (1958). Sylvia Plath's protagonist lands in the same neighbourhood but sells her sanity in place of her soul (*The Bell Jar*, 1963). Wander west into Central Park to wonder about the ducks in winter with *The Catcher in the Rye*'s Holden Caulfield (1951) before Henry Roth introduces you to immigrant life on the Lower East Side (*Call it Sleep*, 1934). The F train takes you to Queens for Korean groceries (Chang-rae Lee's *Native Speaker*, 1995) and south for greenery – both in landscape (Betty Smith's *A Tree Grows in Brooklyn*, 1943) and new beginnings (Colm Toibin's *Brooklyn*, 2009).

RELATED ENTRIES

See also
HARLEM RENAISSANCE
page 124

NEWSPAPERS & MAGAZINES
page 126

NEW YORK ON THE
BIG SCREEN
page 144

3-SECOND BIOGRAPHIES

JOSEPH PULITZER
1847–1911
Hungarian-born publisher whose will established the awards for achievement in music, journalism and literature now overseen by Columbia University

ARTHUR MILLER
1915–2005
Harlem-born playwright of the Pulitzer-Prize winning *Death of a Salesman* (1949)

30-SECOND TEXT

Sarah Fenton

'I love New York, even though it isn't mine'. Truman Capote's sentiment is one shared by authors and readers alike.

MUSEUMS

the 30-second tour

Because New York City has so long served as the nation's gateway for immigrants, the stories told by its heritage and cultural museums are never merely local but national – even international – narratives. Visitors to the Lower East Side's Tenement Museum from as far away as Kansas or Kilkenny might find evidence of their own forbears amidst the steamer trunks, crockery and cherished photographs. Further uptown at the Museum of the City of New York in its current home at Fifth Avenue and 103rd Street clipper ships share the spotlight with colonial furniture and twentieth-century haute couture. The Hispanic Society of America, one of the first museums devoted to ethnic studies, opened in Washington Heights in 1904; just over a century later, the Museum of Chinese in America moved into a Maya Lin-designed building on the border between Chinatown and Little Italy. For immersive experiences of a different sort, climb aboard the former aircraft carrier now docked at Pier 86 (USS *Intrepid*) or head to Queens for the interactive exhibits at its Hall of Science. Equally immersive are the Brooklyn Children's Museum – the first of its kind when it opened in 1899 – and the New York Transit Museum, whose visitors can descend into the tunnels of a decommissioned subway station.

3-SECOND SURVEY
Not content merely to safeguard brontosaurus bones and colonial costumes, today's museum curators research issues as pressing as climate change, species extinction and cultural identity.

3-MINUTE OVERVIEW
Set alongside Central Park on a scenic stretch of the Upper West Side, the American Museum of Natural History wears its cultural and scientific significance with all the confidence of a diva. Inspired by the strides in evolutionary biology made in Charles Darwin's wake, it originated in a small series of collections at the New York Arsenal in 1869 and now boasts more than 32 million specimens of animals, plants, fossils, meteorites and cultural artifacts.

RELATED ENTRIES
See also
THE CITY TAKES SHAPE
page 14

ART: MUSEUMS
page 118

3-SECOND BIOGRAPHIES
DAVID HOSACK
1769–1835
New York-born physician and botanist whose Elgin Botanic Garden heralded the extensive Botanic Gardens now located in Brooklyn and the Bronx

JAMES PERRY WILSON
1889–1976
American artist who painted the AMNH's magnificent animal dioramas, first presented in 1942 and painstakingly restored in 2011

30-SECOND TEXT
Sarah Fenton

Many of the city's best-known museums were established by the industrialists who prospered in the decades following the American Civil War.

SONG, SCREEN & SPORT

SONG, SCREEN & SPORT
GLOSSARY

b-boys Breakdancers. B-boying – also known as 'break-dancing' or 'breaking'– is a form of street dance that originated in the 1970s among African-American and Puerto Rican New Yorkers.

brownstone Type of townhouse, so-called because it is clad in brown sandstone. In New York brownstones are found especially in Brooklyn and the Upper West Side.

cyphers Informal rapping contests.

Knicks New York Knickerbockers, known as the Knicks, a basketball team in the NBA that plays at Madison Square Garden. Their New York rivals in the NBA are the Brooklyn Nets, who play at the Barclays Center, in Brooklyn.

Manolo Blahniks High-end women's shoes by Spanish designer of that name and famously coveted and worn by Carrie Bradshaw (Sarah-Jane Parker) in New York TV show *Sex and the City*.

MCs Alternative name for rappers. 'MC' derives from Master of Ceremonies. The MC controls the microphone and raps over the music.

Mets Major League baseball team located in Queens, founded in 1962 after the Brooklyn Dodgers and the New York Giants moved to Los Angeles and San Francisco, respectively. The Mets played at the celebrated Shea Stadium in Flushing Meadows–Corona Park, Queens, in 1964–2008. Their new ballpark, Citi Field, is on an adjacent site.

New York City Marathon Annual race covering just over 42 km (26 miles) along a course through the five boroughs, starting in Staten Island near the Verrazano Bridge and finishing outside the Tavern on the Green in Central Park. It was first run in 1970.

Savoy Ballroom Ballroom between 140th Street and 141st Street in Harlem, Manhattan, open 1926–58. The 1934 jazz standard 'Stompin' at the Savoy' – covered by greats including Judy Garland, Art Tatum, Ella Fitzgerald and Louis Armstrong – was named after the ballroom.

subway series Ball games between rival New York teams – once Yankees vs. Giants or Yankees vs. Dodgers, today Yankees vs. Mets. Originally the name was applied to games between the rivals in the end-of-season World Series but now it is used for Yankees/Mets clashes in the regular season.

Sugar Hill District in Hamilton Heights, Harlem, so called because it was home to the rich and famous in the 1920s. Bill Strayhorn's jazz standard 'Take the A Train' namechecks Sugar Hill. The Sugarhill Gang – who released 'Rapper's Delight', the first rap single to hit the Top 40 – is named after Sugar Hill.

'Take Me Out to the Ball Game' Tin Pan Alley song from 1908, written in New York by Jack Norworth and Albert Von Tilzer and an unofficial anthem for ball fans. The chorus is traditionally sung in a crowd singalong during the 'seventh inning stretch', the break that takes place between the two halves of the game's seventh inning.

Yankees Iconic Major League baseball team who played at Yankee Stadium – aka 'the Cathedral of Baseball' – in the Bronx in 1923–73 and 1976–2008. In 2009 they moved to a new, $2.3 billion stadium, given the same name, on adjacent land at the corner of River Avenue and 161st Street, also in the Bronx. The Yankees began life as the Baltimore Orioles in 1901–02, then moved to New York and were the New York Highlanders for a decade until they took their current name in 1913.

Queensboro Bridge Bridge across the East River connecting the Long Island City neighbourhood of Queens with Manhattan. In Woody Allen's 1979 movie *Manhattan* Davis (Woody Allen) and Mary Wilkie (Diane Keaton) sit on a bench in Sutton Place Park looking at the bridge at dawn and the image – used on the movie's poster – is now an iconic New York view. The bridge is also known as the 59th Street Bridge because its Manhattan end is between 59th Street and 60th Street, and it is referenced in the 1966 Simon and Garfunkel song 'The 59th Street Bridge Song (Feelin' Groovy)'.

CLASSICAL CITY

the 30-second text

How do you get to Carnegie Hall?

'Practise, practise, practise!' goes the famous joke. Since Tchaikovsky opened Carnegie in 1891 with a concert of his own works, musicians the world over have set their sights on playing this stage. It's the city's most hallowed hall of classical music, next to Lincoln Center – the largest performing arts centre anywhere. This 6.5-hectare (16-acre) campus is home to a dozen performance companies and music educational institutions – most notably, the Metropolitan Opera and New York Philharmonic. These companies retain avid local audiences and are major tourist attractions, but seek to serve the globe, as well. The Philharmonic makes radio broadcasts and has its own recording label, while the Met Opera produces HD telecasts that are transmitted to more than 2,000 movie theatres in 70 countries. New Yorkers don't just take their Verdi and Chopin in vast, chandelier-lit auditoriums, though. They head to Bargemusic, a renovated coffee barge moored in the East River under the Brooklyn Bridge for intimate chamber concerts. And on summer nights, with tens of thousands of their neighbours, they tuck blankets and baguettes under their arms to sprawl out on the Great Lawn of Central Park and watch the Philharmonic perform free concerts, capped off with firework shows.

3-SECOND SURVEY
Until you've heard Tchaikovsky's *Fifth* or *West Side Story* in Central Park – as have millions of New Yorkers since 1965 – you haven't heard them at all.

3-MINUTE OVERVIEW
While not Vienna or Berlin, New York has nurtured many renowned classical musicians. Antonín Dvořák composed his New World Symphony here. Brooklynites Aaron Copland ('Dean of American Music') and George Gershwin (famous on Broadway but also for opera and concertos – think of *Porgy and Bess* or *Rhapsody in Blue*) together with Leonard Bernstein popularized classical music for the American public. Meanwhile, East Villager Philip Glass has transformed classical music and opera today with his minimalist works.

RELATED ENTRY
See also
NEW YORK'S TOP 40
page 140

3-SECOND BIOGRAPHIES
LEONARD BERNSTEIN
1918–90
Conductor of the New York Philharmonic 1958–90, classical, pop and jazz composer best known for *West Side Story*

BEVERLY SILLS
1929–2007
Opera star and TV personality, began her career as 'house soprano' at the City Opera of New York in 1955, then became its general director; later chaired both the Lincoln Center and the Metropolitan Opera

30-SECOND TEXT
Jennifer Shalant

Leonard Bernstein embodied New York certitude: 'I'm no longer quite sure what the question is, but I do know that the answer is Yes.'

NEW YORK'S TOP 40

the 30-second tour

3-SECOND SURVEY
Defined by and defining the city, music has always been central to the cultural growth of New York.

Wake up in a city that never sleeps, give your regards to Broadway, take the A train to Sugar Hill, walk down streets that make you feel brand-new – and never lose your New York State of Mind. Everyone from John Lennon to Frank Sinatra, Billie Holiday to Alicia Keys has belted out their valentine to this city. In turn those musical love letters define this city, which is the birthplace of so many genres – hip hop, bebop, punk, disco, Latin jazz – a mix that could only emerge here. And the beat goes on . . . and on. 'New York, New York' is played over the loudspeakers at the start of every New York City Marathon and at the end of every Yankees game. The songs get reinvented, too, passed down, resampled and rerecorded. Today – better yet, this weekend – ride the subway east in the wee hours of the morning and some rowdy group will be shouting 'No Sleep Til' Brooklyn', the Beastie Boys' 1986 anthem that still captures the raw energy of a New York night out.

3-MINUTE OVERVIEW
New York's Top 40 is not all pomp and circumstance. The city's songbook is full of lyrics that capture its grit, from jazz standards such as Billie Holiday's 'Autumn in New York' to the alienation found in Simon and Garfunkel's folk classic 'Sound of Silence', to Lou Reed's ode to the junkie life in 'I'm Waiting for My Man' and the narrative of inner-city violence underlying the Grandmaster Flash hip-hop track 'The Message.'

RELATED ENTRY
See also
CLASSICAL CITY
page 138

3-SECOND BIOGRAPHIES
FRANK SINATRA
1915–98
Foremost singer of the American songbook (also, actor, producer and director), and one of the best-selling musicians of all time, with more than 150 million records sold worldwide

ELLA FITZGERALD
1917–96
Jazz singer known as the 'First Lady of Song', who sung with all the jazz greats from Duke Ellington to Benny Goodman, and packed concert halls from Harlem's Savoy Ballroom to Carnegie Hall

30-SECOND TEXT
Jennifer Shalant

Duke Ellington defied music critics looking to label his sound, saying that it was 'beyond category' — part of the melting pot of American music.

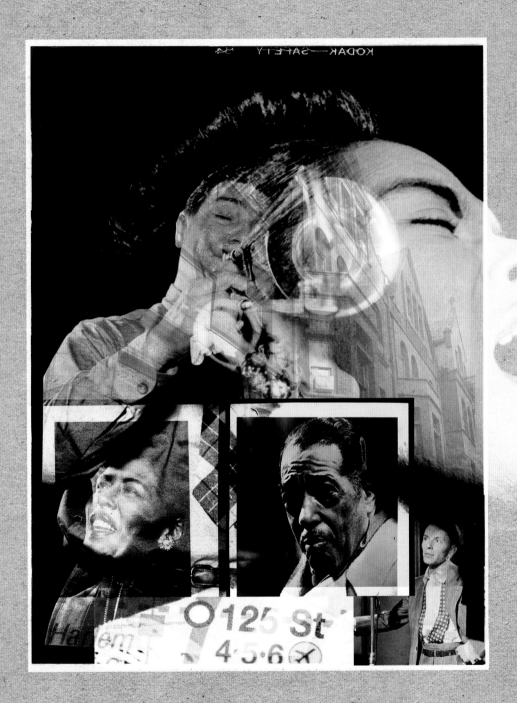

4 December 1969
Born in Bedford-Stuyvesant, Brooklyn

1974
Moves to Marcy Projects

1989
Appears on Jaz-O's 'Hawaiian Sophie'

1994
Featured on Big Daddy Kane's album *Daddy's Home*

1996
Founds Roc-a-Fella Records in New York

1996
Releases debut album *Reasonable Doubt*

1999
Launches Hard Knock Life Tour, creates Rocawear clothing line

2001
Hits number one on *Billboard* 200 with *The Blueprint*

2003
Announces 'retirement' with *The Black Album*

2004
Named president of Def Jam Records

2005–2007
Releases *Kingdom Come* and *American Gangster*

2008
Marries Beyoncé, founds Roc Nation

2011
Collaborates with Kanye West on *Watch the Throne*

2012
Samples newborn Blue on 'Glory', brings the Nets to Brooklyn

2013
Releases *Magna Carta Holy Grail*, launches Roc Nation Sports

2015
Purchases music-streaming service Tidal

JAY Z

When he was six, Shawn Carter (now better known as Jay Z) moved from his grandmother's brownstone on Lexington Avenue to a six-storey apartment building in Bedford-Stuyvesant, Brooklyn. It was here, in the Marcy Projects, that Jay Z was first introduced to hip-hop culture. DJs ran extension cords from building basements to paved courtyards, mixing disco, soul and R&B. Local MCs battled in front of raucous crowds. B-boys swiped and spun on sheets of linoleum. The neighbourhood recognized Jay-Z's talents from an early age. He kept his family up late banging out beats on the kitchen table. He held his own in high-school cyphers with classmates Busta Rhymes and Biggie Smalls. He earned cameos on early 1990s albums by local mentors Big Daddy Kane and Jaz-O.

But Jay Z had no luck getting signed by a record label, and put increasing energy into dealing drugs, orchestrating a supply chain between New Jersey, East New York and Baltimore. By the time record companies tried signing him Jay Z had acquired enough capital to start his own record company, Roc-a-Fella Records.

Outside of industry channels, Roc-a-Fella records self-marketed two hit songs before cutting the album *Reasonable Doubt* in 1996. An unprecedented string of hits followed, from 'Hard Knock Life' in 1998 to *The Black Album* in 2003. Record sales were only the tip of the Roc-a-Fella iceberg: the Hard Knock Life Tour profited $18 million in 11 weeks; Rocawear clothing cleared $700 million in annual sales; the 40/40 Club opened multiple locations. Considered a master of flow by rap aficionados, Jay Z's legacy might well be defined as much for business acumen as lyrical prowess. 'I'm not a businessman,' he explained in 2005, 'I'm a business, man.'

Jay Z moved on to become CEO and president of Def Jam Records while simultaneously releasing *Kingdom Come* and *American Gangster*, campaigning for presidential nominee Barack Obama, appearing on two Beyoncé albums, and, in April 2008, marrying his musical collaborator.

Cementing himself as one of the world's most ambitious entrepreneurs, Jay Z founded Live Nation and J Hotels, produced a Broadway musical, bought a stake in the Brooklyn Nets, helped bring the Barclay's Center to downtown Brooklyn, launched a sports agency firm (Roc Nation Sports) and acquired controlling share of the music-streaming service Tidal. He also started a family, welcoming Blue Ivy Carter into the world in January 2012. Her cries, recorded at the end of 'Glory', make B.I.C. the youngest artist ever to be credited on Billboard charts.

Patrick Nugent

NEW YORK ON THE BIG SCREEN

the 30-second tour

3-SECOND SURVEY
Moviegoers love seeing the city under siege, whether by apes (*King Kong*, 1933), paranormal activity (*Ghostbusters*, 1984), aliens (*Independence Day*, 1996) or monsters (*Cloverfield*, 2008).

3-MINUTE OVERVIEW
In October 1888, Thomas Edison professed to be 'experimenting upon an instrument which does for the Eye what the phonograph does for the Ear'. Edison first exhibited his 'motion pictures' in May 1893 at the Brooklyn Institute. The early twentieth century saw nickelodeons – storefront theatres that charged a nickle (5 cents) and housed a projector, screen, piano and cluster of camp chairs – multiply across New York City just as the film industry migrated west to Hollywood.

Those who know New York only from the movies could be forgiven for thinking that music teachers (*An Affair to Remember*, 1957) and struggling actors (*Rosemary's Baby*, 1968) occupy vast apartments with park views. Film buffs who imagine Times Square as either the stuff of dreams (*42nd Street*, 1933) or nightmares (*Taxi Driver*, 1976) might be surprised to find merely a garish commercial intersection. New Yorkers off-screen may bear little resemblance to the beguiling creatures in *Rear Window* (Grace Kelly, 1954) and *Breakfast at Tiffany's* (Audrey Hepburn, 1961). But nor do they behave with the wanton villainy of Gordon Gekko (*Wall Street*, 1987) or Patrick Bateman (*American Psycho*, 2000). And however lovingly Woody Allen films his city, no screen can improve upon the Queensboro Bridge seen from a bench at Sutton Place Park (*Manhattan*, 1979). On the other hand, one could do worse than learn subway etiquette from *The Taking of Pelham 123* (1974): keep your cool when the guns come out. Beware both the sharp wit of a fading Broadway star (*All About Eve*, 1950) and building tensions in Bed-Stuy on a hot summer's day (*Do the Right Thing*, 1989). And newly arrived strivers can in fact be found prowling Fifth Avenue with hope in their eyes and heartbreak in their futures (*Midnight Cowboy*, 1969).

RELATED ENTRIES
See also
LITERARY CITY:
NEW YORK STORIES
page 130

NEW YORK'S TOP 40
page 140

THE SMALL SCREEN
page 146

3-SECOND BIOGRAPHIES
PAULINE KAEL
1919–2001
Idiosyncratic and enormously influential film critic for *The New Yorker* magazine from 1968 to 1991

MARTIN SCORSESE
1942–
Italian-American filmmaker from Queens, whose eight Academy Award nominations make him the most nominated living director

30-SECOND TEXT
Sarah Fenton

'Movie Palaces' reached the peak of luxury in the 1920s with swanky ushers, live orchestras and extravagant architecture.

THE SMALL SCREEN

the 30-second tour

3-SECOND SURVEY
New York is at once
ridiculous, glamorous,
gritty and smart, capturing
the imagination of viewers,
launching a thousand
trends and making for
addictive entertainment.

3-SECOND SURVEY
New York is at once
ridiculous, glamorous,
gritty and smart, capturing
the imagination of viewers,
launching a thousand
trends and making for
addictive entertainment.

3-MINUTE OVERVIEW
'If you're not gonna be a
part of a civil society, then
just get in your car and
drive on over to the East
Side' (*Seinfeld*); 'Beauty is
fleeting, but a rent-
controlled apartment
overlooking the park is
forever' (*Sex and the
City*); 'Don's in advertising
. . . No way. Madison
Avenue? What a gas!' (*Mad
Men*); 'This is New York,
remember? Sometimes
people get beat up just for
the hell of it' (*Law and
Order*); 'Live from New
York, it's Saturday night!'
(*Saturday Night Live*)

If television is to be trusted,

Manhattan is brimming with hard-boiled
criminals, unfrozen cavemen lawyers, close-
talkers, tortured advertising executives and
more Manolo Blahniks than can fit into a
rent-stabilized brownstone. In *Seinfeld*,
Jerry, Kramer, George and Elaine endure the
absurdities of everyday New York populated by
soup Nazis, low-talkers, double-dippers and
developers of manssieres – bras for men, not
that there's anything wrong with that. In *Sex
and the City*, New York glittered with designer
boutiques and trendy restaurants. A candid look
at sex and friendship, it had us sorting ourselves
as a Carrie, Miranda, Charlotte or Samantha, and
debating Mr. Big vs. Aidan. *Law & Order*, the
gritty police procedural/legal drama, was filmed
on the city's mean streets, with plots ripped
from the headlines, generous splashes of
local colour and cameos from hometown
personalities such as politician Rudy Giuliani
and author Fran Lebowitz. *Saturday Night
Live* parodied politics and pop culture, set the
stage for scads of famous alumi, and gave us
hundreds of quotable characters, earning a
record 45 Emmys and countless laughs. Today
there are 46 shows filming in New York, proving
it's one city that's always camera-ready.

RELATED ENTRIES
See also
NEW YORK'S TOP 40
page 140

NEW YORK ON THE BIG
SCREEN
page 144

3-SECOND BIOGRAPHIES
JACKIE GLEASON
1916–87
American actor and comedian,
starred as bus-driver
Ralph Kramden in *The
Honeymooners*, set in
Bushwick, Brooklyn, and one
of the first shows to depict
working-class Americans

JIM HENSON
1936–90
Puppeteer famous for the
Muppets and a 20-year
collaboration with the PBS
show set on the fictional
Manhattan lane, *Sesame Street*

30-SECOND TEXT
Cheong Kim

*New York City was the
heart of television
until the 1950s, when
it was displaced by
Hollywood. It still
remains the centre
of network news.*

THE CONTACT SPORTS

the 30-second text

On 21 November 1905 Union

College sophomore and defensive back Harold Moore tackled a New York University lineman. Helmetless and crushed under a scrum of bodies, Moore died of a cerebral haemorrhage. He was one of three players to die that day and one of 20 that year from football injuries, prompting President Roosevelt to summon a selection of coaches to the White House to set some guidelines. Their summit produced rules permitting forward passes and stopping play once the ball was down, eliminating the kind of pile-up that buried Moore. Helmets would not become mandatory for another three decades. But New Yorkers love their gridiron gladiators and boast two teams in the National Football League. The Jets and Giants share a stadium (in East Rutherford, New Jersey) and one of the biggest markets in professional sports. The waiting list for Giants season tickets surpasses 125,000 names – they are the league's oldest Northeastern team, hold the record for most championship berths, and have four Super Bowl titles. In the Jets' lone Super Bowl appearance (in 1969), quarterback Joe Namath made good on his guarantee to defeat the much favoured Baltimore Colts. Theories abound as to how New Yorkers choose which team to support, from geography to class to family tradition.

3-SECOND SURVEY

Brutality is not unique to football, and basketball alone does not rule the Garden: New York also has two teams in the National Hockey League.

3-MINUTE OVERVIEW

Though first played in Massachusetts, basketball's true home is New York City: from cramped asphalt playgrounds to sweaty college gymnasiums to nights at Madison Square Garden when the Knickerbockers are on fire – and the crowd is, too. The Garden has also been home court to the New York Liberty since the founding of the Women's Basketball Association in 1996. The Brooklyn Nets moved into their Barclay's Center home on hip and hopping Atlantic Avenue in 2012.

RELATED ENTRIES

See also
THEODORE ROOSEVELT
page 24

EDUCATING THE CITY
page 112

PLAY BALL!
page 150

3-SECOND BIOGRAPHIES

LAWRENCE TAYLOR
1959–
The best defensive player in football history, spent his entire career as a linebacker for the New York Giants, with whom he won two Super Bowls

MARK MESSIER
1961–
Captained the team and scored the winning goal in Game 7 of the Stanley Cup Finals at Madison Square Garden in 1994, giving the Rangers their first Stanley Cup in 54 years

30-SECOND TEXT
Sarah Fenton

The NBA, founded in New York City in 1946, was slow to integrate. Today, nearly three quarters of its players are African American.

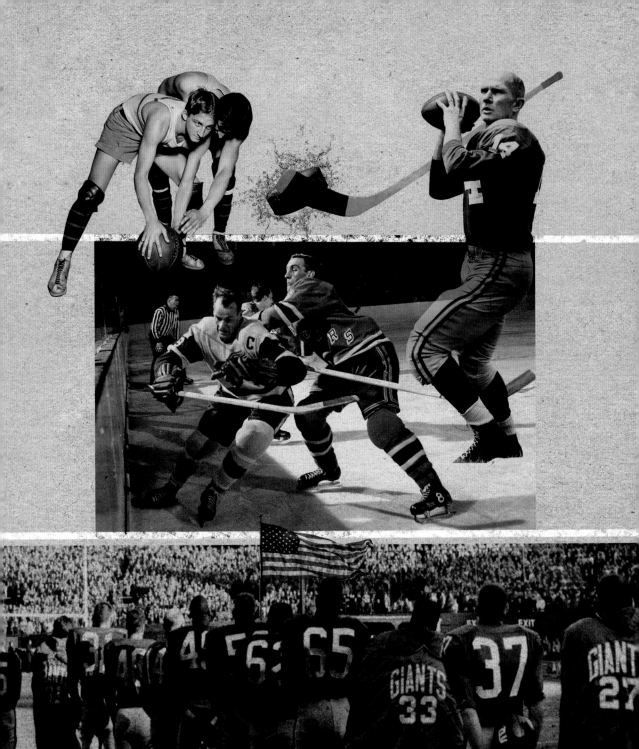

PLAY BALL!

the 30-second text

Few things bring New Yorkers together more than a subway series, the annual face-off between its pro baseball teams. Residents of the concrete jungle need a physical outlet, or at least a place to yell and cheer. Luckily there's plenty to choose from, with six pro teams playing within the city limits. Baseball claims the biggest fan base and most New Yorkers take sides, supporting either the perennial champions, the 'Bronx Bombers' (Yankees) or their interleague (underdog) rivals, the Mets. These loyalties have deep roots. When the Brooklyn Dodgers and New York Giants – neither of which could ever top the Yanks – left for California in 1957, their orphaned fans transferred allegiances to the replacement team. The Mets have reinforced this legacy with their new ballpark, Citi Field, modelled on the Dodgers' one-time home at Ebbets Field. Citi Field's Jackie Robinson Rotunda honours the former Dodger who broke ground in 1947 as the first African American to play major-league baseball. In addition to legends on the field, New York has spawned many sports figures better known for their voices. It claims the country's first 24-hour sports talk station, WFAN, and for generations its famed radio broadcasters have touched millions of listeners with their play-by-play announcements.

3-SECOND SURVEY
The anthem of baseball, 'Take Me Out to the Ball Game', came out of (you guessed it) New York City – penned on a subway ride.

3-MINUTE OVERVIEW
New York's streets were once the turf of kids with sports gear such as pink rubber 'spaldeens' and broomsticks for stickball (with manholes as bases) and bottlecaps and chalk for a pavement-drawn board game called 'skelly' or 'skully'. Stickball took off in the early twentieth century. During its heyday in the 1940s–50s, there was a stickball team on every block of some neighbourhoods, from Spanish Harlem to Little Italy.

RELATED ENTRIES
See also
THE BRONX
page 16

AFRICAN AMERICANS IN NEW YORK
page 40

3-SECOND BIOGRAPHIES
GEORGE HERMAN 'BABE' RUTH JR.
1895–1948
An outfielder for the New York Yankees who set records for home runs; considered the greatest baseball player of the twentieth century

WILLIE HOWARD MAYS JR
1931–
Longtime star of the New York Giants who grew up playing in the Negro League of the Deep South; recipient of the 2015 Presidential Medal of Freedom

30-SECOND TEXT
Jennifer S halant

New York poet Walt Whitman christened baseball 'the American game', believing it had 'the snap, go, fling, of the American atmosphere.'

APPENDICES

NOTES ON CONTRIBUTORS

CONSULTANT EDITOR

Sarah Fenton began working on this book from an apartment in Stuyvesant Town – Manhattan's friendliest neighbourhood, scandalously under covered here – while her children attended two of New York City's finest public schools: PS 40 and School of the Future. A historian of the nineteenth-century United States, Sarah has taught at Lake Forest College, the Newberry Library and Northwestern University, where she earned a doctorate in history in 2004. After many years of research and editorial work for the *Encyclopedia of Chicago*, Sarah became Contributing Editor to the *American Historical Association*, where she writes for *Perspectives* magazine and *AHA Today*.

WRITERS

Andrew Kryzak was prepared at Hotchkiss and studied at Duke and Columbia. A native New Yorker, he has worked for the *Encyclopedia of New York City* and the New-York Historical Society. He is a graduate Divinity student at Yale University. His academic and personal interests include Western history; sacred music; Classical and Gothic architecture; detective fiction; and the city of New York.

Cheong Kim has a background as diverse as her writing. She has developed numerous restaurants in Chicago, managed digital communities for high profile food and beverage companies, and spent 10 years marketing books for Random House and

Penguin Putnam in New York City. In 2015 she traveled the world, visiting 62 cities in 21 countries with her family, which she documented on her blog, *Wrinkled: Adventures in Travel, Writing and Aging Gracefully*. She holds a degree from Sarah Lawrence College with a concentration in poetry and fiction writing.

Jennifer Shalant is a lifelong New Yorker and serves as director of digital marketing at the Museum of the City of New York. She holds an MS from the Columbia Graduate School of Journalism. In addition to chronicling the stories of the city, she had also written about environmental issues for the Wildlife Conservation Society, Natural Resources Defense Council, and American Museum of Natural History. She lives with her husband and two young sons in the Hudson River Valley just north of New York City.

Christopher Mitchell is an adjunct professor of women's, gender and sexuality studies at Hunter College. He also teaches United States and queer history at Rutgers University-Newark and men and masculinities at Pace University. He holds a BA in English and history from Texas Tech University.

Patrick Nugent is the Deputy Director of the C. V. Starr Center for the Study of the American Experience at Washington College. There, he teaches environmental and cultural studies in addition to spearheading public history projects on the shores of the Chesapeake Bay. His dissertation, 'The Urban Environmental Order: Planning and Politics in New York City's "Last Frontier"' traces the interconnected histories of civil rights and environmentalism on Staten Island. Prior to his PhD studies, Dr Nugent taught urban and environmental literature at Brooklyn College while leading historical bicycle tours through New York City.

Matthew Gordon Lasner is associate professor of urban studies and planning at Hunter College, CUNY. He is author of *High Life: Condo Living in the Suburban Century* and co-editor of *Affordable Housing in New York: The Places, People, and Policies That Transformed a City*. His research explores the production of metropolitan space with particular focus on housing and the relationship between dwelling patterns, social change and urban and suburban form. He earned his PhD in architecture from Harvard.

Nancy Green Saraisky is a Research Associate at Teachers College, Columbia University. Her research and teaching interests focus on education policy and politics, both domestically and internationally. Prior to her work in education, she held a variety of positions in journalism, philanthropy and government. Nancy holds a PhD from Columbia University, an MSc from the London School of Economics and a BA from Tufts University.

Aaron Shkuda is an urban historian and the author of *The Lofts of SoHo: Gentrification, Art, and Industry in New York, 1950–1980*. His work has been published in the *Journal of Urban History* and the *Journal of Planning History*. Aaron has taught courses in history, urban studies and the arts at Princeton, Stanford, Carnegie Mellon and the University of Chicago. He is currently the Project Manager of the Princeton-Mellon Initiative in Architecture, Urbanism and the Humanities.

Chris McNickle is the author of *To Be Mayor of New York: Ethnic Politics in the City, The Power of the Mayor: David Dinkins 1990-1993*, and *Bloomberg: A Billionaire's Ambition*. He holds a B.A. in economics and international relations from the University of Pennsylvania and a PhD in United States history from the University of Chicago. He lives in New York City where he writes about local politics and history.

Michael Willoughby is a writer and editor whom love took to New York City in 1998. While doing PR for web site start-ups, he found himself at the heart of that city's gay elite and enjoyed its highly specific culture and nightlife. As such, he saw New York at its highest point and, after 9/11, its lowest. Today he lives in London's East End with his husband, mostly writing about buildings. He is currently editing a fable about the perils of being an oil economy for an Iraqi artist.

RESOURCES

BOOKS

Collected Essays
James Baldwin
(1998)

The Power Broker
Robert Caro
(1974)

Gay New York
George Chauncey
(1995)

Alexander Hamilton
Ron Chernow
(2004)

Through the Children's Gate
Adam Gopnik
(2007)

The Mambo Kings Play Songs of Love
Oscar Hijuelos
(1989)

Huxtable On Architecture
Ada Louise Huxtable
(2008)

The Encyclopedia of New York City
Kenneth T. Jackson
(1995)

The Death and Life of Great American Cities
Jane Jacobs
(1961)

The Boys of Summer
Roger Kahn
(1972)

Amusing the Million
John Kasson
(1978)

Delirious New York
Rem Koolhaas
(1978)

How the Other Half Lives
Jacob Riis
(1890)

M Train
Patti Smith
(2015)

City of Women
Christine Stansell
(1989)

The Devil's Playground
James Traub
(2004)

The Andy Warhol Diaries
Andy Warhol
(1989)

Here is New York
E. B. White
(1949)

WEBSITES

www.metmuseum.org

www.moma.org

www.newyorker.com

www.nytimes.com

www.whitney.org

INDEX

ACKNOWLEDGEMENTS

Sarah Fenton would like to thank her colleagues at the American Historical Association as well as her parents, husband and children – each of them New Yorkers at different moments in their own and the city's history.

The publisher would like to thank the following for permission to reproduce copyright material:
All images from Shutterstock, Inc./www.shutterstock.com and Clipart Images/www.clipart.com unless stated.

Getty Images/ Hulton Archive: 37; Allan Tannenbaum: 59; George Rinhart: 87; New York Daily News Archive: 97, 109, 149; Fred W. McDarrah: 103; Bettmann: 109, 147; Genevieve Naylor: 121; Ben Van Meerondonk: 121; Constantin Joffe: 131; Alfred Eisenstaedt: 84.

Library of Congress, Washington D.C.: 17, 19, 21, 41, 43, 45, 53, 55, 57, 60, 63, 79, 87, 89, 95, 98, 101, 103, 109, 113, 121, 123, 125, 127, 141, 147, 151.

Mary Evans Picture Library/INTERFOTO AGENTUR: 145; Everett Collection: 149.

NASA: 29.

The New York Public Library: 15, 17, 19, 21, 23, 27, 35, 41, 45, 53, 55, 63, 71, 73, 75, 77, 81, 83, 87, 95, 97, 103, 109, 113, 121, 123, 125, 139, 147, 151.

Wikipedia/Fletcher6: 47; BeyondMyKen: 119.

All reasonable efforts have been made to trace copyright holders and to obtain their permission for the use of copyright material. The publisher apologizes for any errors or omissions in the list above and will gratefully incorporate any corrections in future reprints if notified.